PROPERTY TRENDSETTERS

Inspirational Property Experts Share
Their Journeys to Success

POWERHOUSE PUBLICATIONS

Copyright

Powerhouse Publications
Suite 124
94 London Road
Headington
Oxford
OX3 9FN

WWW.POWERHOUSEPUBLISHING.COM

CONTENTS

INTRODUCTION

Have you ever thought about investing in property? But when you look into it, you feel daunted. It feels like there are too many strategies to learn. Your friends and family warn you it's "risky". The newspapers are full of doom and gloom. You wonder how you'll find the money to invest. Or what will happen if things go wrong...

Or maybe you're investing in property already, but you're facing challenges. You're wondering how other successful property experts cope with sourcing finances, organizing joint ventures, or dealing with difficult tenants. You wonder what they do to overcome the hurdles.

It's easy to imagine that successful property experts started from a different place to you. That they had access to some secret knowledge that you don't possess. That they had more money when they got started. That they had "contacts" who helped them. That things never went wrong for them and everything ran smoothly. Or that they just struck lucky.

In this book, you'll discover the stories of men and women from all walks of life. You'll find out why they decided to get started in property investing, how they took their first steps, and what they did along the way to make create their success. You'll hear the inspiring stories of:

- A single mother who was turned away from the Benefits Office as she hadn't paid enough contributions.
- The businessmen who were £150,000 pounds in debt, with their backs against the wall.
- A soldier about to be sent to Afghanistan, who wanted to quit the army.
- A housewife who had let her husband manage their finances for 18 years, and considered herself dyslexic with numbers.
- A police officer who was pensioned out of her job after being injured on duty.
- The father of a young baby who quit his 'safe' job because he was tired of his employer telling him what to do.
- A mother working crazy hours, not seeing enough of her kids – and still knowing she wouldn't have a big enough pension.
- And many more...

You see, people come to property from many different starting points – and often, it is desperation that enables them to push past their fears and step outside their comfort zone. Failure is simply not an option.

You may wonder what you need to do to get started on your own property journey. What should you focus on first? What are the steps that you need to take? What are the mistakes to avoid? What are the shortcuts to get you there faster?

In this book, you'll discover the steps that others took to go from "beginner" to successful property expert. You'll learn from their experiences and discover a few shortcuts to help you on your own journey.

The men and women you're about to meet in this book have all been exactly where you are now – which is to say, they started with little or no knowledge. But they overcame their trepidation, and pushed ahead anyway.

We'll follow these property experts through the early decisions that helped set them on their property paths and look at what they did to overcome any obstacles they faced. We'll discover their biggest aha moments, their failures, and the achievements they are most proud of.

And the good news? If they can do it, you can achieve this too.

I hope you'll be inspired by their stories.

Stephanie J. Hale
Powerhouse Publications

BELINDA GRASHION

Start from where you are with what you have ...
and make that start Today

Belinda Grashion is an entrepreneur with over 20 years' experience in property investment, trading, training, and mentoring.

She offers a wide range of programmes and services—from buying your first investment property to investing in multi-million-pound developments—and offers her expertise, skills, and knowledge to assist others.

Belinda Grashion specializes in helping beginners achieve financial freedom.

After a successful career in property, development, and investments, she now mentors others to achieve the same success, so they can stop trading time for money and go on to enjoy life to the full.

Belinda Grashion is no stranger to being a beginner. She spent 18 years as a housewife and mother before becoming a single mother on benefits and starting from the very beginning to get where she is today.

Business: Property investment and trading company. Property educational training programme.

Services offered: Different levels of property education to help people become financially free so that they have time, money, and freedom. Assistance via video tutorials, hand-held support, and weekly calls.

Email: info@belindagrashion.com

Tel: 01302 965141

Website: www.belindagrashion.com

*

When I was first asked to be a part of this book, I was humbled and flattered. But I must admit, it made me reflect on what it was that qualified me for the title of Property Trendsetter.

I certainly never used to think of myself as a trendsetter. But then I never used to believe I could be successful either (in property, or anything else for that matter), and after some reflection, I realized that was it!

The trend I'm setting in the property industry is that I'm inspiring women who may not believe they fit the profile of a successful property investor to believe in themselves, take charge of their financial future, and create a life of freedom, meaning, and purpose with property—no matter their circumstances might look like to begin with.

What I know, and what I'm living proof of, is that it truly does not matter what background you come from or how many times you've 'failed' in the past. The only thing that matters is that you start where you are and that you never, ever give up. That is the only thing that can ever stop you from creating the success you want in life. Nobody else can stop you. And no circumstances can stop you. Only giving up can.

I hope that by sharing my story, I can help you to see that I don't have any special powers that you don't have. I've created the success I enjoy today with the powers we ALL have as women— powers that do indeed give us a huge advantage in this business (like being heart-centred, intuitive, and driven to do whatever it takes for the people we love). But again, we ALL share these powers. The fact that I have created so much success in my life means that you can too.

All you have to do is start where you are and never, ever give up.

Yes, there may well be tears along the way. There certainly were for me. But what's waiting for you on the other side of those tears is a life of true freedom, meaning, and purpose. A life where you get to do the things you really want to do with the people you love the most, AND where you get to make an incredible contribution to the people and causes you love the most. If you are a woman who dreams of creating the financial freedom to live a bigger life, but you feel like you don't 'fit the mold' of a successful property investor, I dedicate my story to you and look forward to toasting your success in years to come!

From the very beginning of my life I never felt like I fitted in.

I grew up, along with my three sisters, as part of a very strict religion that I never really felt fitted me very well and, to make matters worse, my dad was in the army so we moved around a lot. There was never much time to settle into a community and feel part of it, and to be honest, I don't really remember much about my school life until the point my dad finally left the army when I was around 12 years of age.

At that point, my family settled down in a council house and my sisters and I went to a local school. I enjoyed going to school but I wasn't very academic. My report card always read, "could do better", but it didn't really matter.

I didn't have any big dreams about what I would do when I left school because my mum controlled us with the religion. We knew from a very young age that we only really had one path, which was to get a job and serve God.

Despite the fact that I didn't really have many aspirations or goals for my life after school, I liked the environment and enjoyed learning new things, even if I disliked a lot of the subjects. However, once again, I didn't really feel like I fitted in for all sorts of reasons.

Because of our religion, my sisters and I weren't allowed to go into school assemblies. The teachers would make us stand outside while everybody else attended, so naturally everybody would look at us strangely and wonder why we were just standing there and not joining in.

Outside of school we were not allowed to associate with other kids either, so again I felt isolated and not part of the community. Let me tell you, being separated from other children in this way can really affect how you react to and interact with others.

Then there were the differences in the way my family lived compared to the families of the other children at school. Every Saturday, my family would go out knocking on doors, trying to talk to people about the Bible—and the reaction was not always a positive one. Some people wouldn't bother answering the door and some would shut it in my face. Others would be downright hostile.

As unenjoyable as this was, if there's one thing I learnt from the experience, it was to not take things personally. It was tough but character building, and little by little I grew into a happy child overall. Don't get me wrong, I certainly wouldn't recommend it to anyone else, but we did have some good times within the religious community.

The village where we lived was very male-dominated. All the men worked down the pit or went to work in the factory, and most of the women went to work in offices. My mum made sure I learnt typing at school so I didn't have to go to the factory because the workers there swore too much.

We never spoke about career progression—it was always about how we could better serve God, so I had no aspirations or dreams about my future. I'd been raised in a way that curbed all those inner desires and dreams.

However, my parents always worked very hard to provide for us. We always felt loved and cared for, although we were not well off materially.

After the army, my dad went to work in the factory and my mum cleaned houses. My mum tried to provide everything she could for us, but she was on a very limited income and we always had to make ends meet and just get by.

I ended up leaving school early, and I never even took my maths exam because I knew I wouldn't pass. I'm terrible with numbers to the point I would call myself dyslexic with them; to this day I still can't do my times tables even though I deal with millions of pounds and I am a whiz with a calculator!

At the age of 15 I left school and went to a recruitment agency to start working. My first sales job was a wonderful experience because I was taken under the wing of a female entrepreneur.

I never had a problem picking up that phone, calling people, and trying to find out how to move them forward. I didn't take no for an answer and was a natural at sales (perhaps this was another positive that came out of my years of knocking on doors).

Even though I was on a low wage because I didn't value myself enough to ask for more, I stayed in this job for about 18 months and loved every moment of it.

That was the first time I saw what someone could achieve through hard work. My boss had her own home, a car, holidays, independence, and freedom. It was a small business so there were only three of us on the team, but it was nice—a completely different environment from what I'd seen or experienced before—and it planted a seed in me. I started to think about different things, and that was the first time I began wanting to leave the religion, because I finally realised how restricted I had been, even in my thinking.

When I was 17, I left home, left the religion behind, rented a tiny little flat, and went to work in a garage. At this point I had never had a boyfriend or even kissed a boy, but I fell in love with the director of the garage. He was 14 years my senior and he swept me off my feet.

To cut a long story short, I got pregnant and, not knowing what to do, I went home. One of the conditions of my being allowed back home was that I had to start attending the religious meetings again. Being only 18, pregnant, and totally overwhelmed, I agreed, and that's where I stayed for another 20 years.

Fortunately, the garage director was in love with me and we got married. I became a housewife and mother to two daughters, and he became an elder in the religious organisation so even more obligations were expected of me. I had to answer at meetings, be on the ministry team, set a good example, be the perfect mother and wife, and keep the home and children clean. Anything financial was left to my husband.

Over the years, the restrictions and obligations only grew. It's funny because as a child I'd always suffered with asthma, but it wasn't until after I read one of Louise Hay's books at the age of 29 that I realised asthma was related to feeling smothered and restricted in your life! I decided I was going to leave the religion once again, but I didn't manage it straight away. It took me another 10 years of suffering with asthma before I finally decided enough was enough, and that I was going to once and for all get out of the religion that made me feel so smothered and restricted.

All those years, I knew I was in the wrong place, and yet I stayed there, not knowing how I could be anywhere or anything else. Your mind will always pull you back towards what is most familiar to you. Even if it's something that doesn't make you happy, if it's what you've been conditioned into it will feel safe there. That's why, when you want to change your life, it's important to stretch your comfort zone and to practice thinking and being a different way until that becomes what's familiar instead.

Anyway, back to my story...

My husband, daughters, and I were living in Tenerife when I eventually left him and came back to the UK with nothing more than two suitcases and my two girls. With the religion I was in, when you leave, you leave everybody—even family and close friends—so I knew I was on my own. To this day, no one has ever phoned me once. Nothing.

I remember getting on that plane crying silently—the tears were almost peacefully rolling down my face. I felt release because I knew I would never set foot in another religious meeting. I had left all those restrictions behind and now the future was my own.

On the one hand I felt total relief, but on the other I was deeply troubled. In 20 years, I'd neither paid nor even seen a bill, I didn't know how much anything cost, I didn't know what would happen, and had no answers. My sister, who was never well off herself and was very ill at the time, had a spare bedroom and put a mattress on the floor for me and the girls to sleep on until I could afford to rent something for myself.

It was months before I was able to move out of my sister's spare bedroom. A friend of my sister was moving down south and said that I could rent their house. It came fully equipped—pots, pans, and everything my girls and I would need. Yet even with my benefits I was short every month, and I wanted things to change.

I knew after watching my dad work in a factory for years—running all the machines and running himself ragged to make ends meet—there had to be a better way. I started looking around and noticing who had the most free time, because that's what I was really after: time and freedom. After all the restriction in my past, I valued freedom most of all.

I noticed again and again that people in property had what I was looking for. Then one day, I noticed an ad in the newspaper about a property course in London. It was a property course from an American man and it was £1,000! I didn't have a penny to my name but I knew I had to attend. It was a sign that I just could not ignore.

So, I applied for a credit card and put the course on that. I was determined to attend. Even if I got there and had nowhere to sleep, I knew I could sit somewhere and stay awake for the two days.

The course really lit a fire in my belly that I just knew would never go out. I didn't understand a lot of what was said because I'd not dealt with anything financial before. Most of what they were saying went right over my head, but I did understand that if you bought something and added value or improved it then you'd get a higher price for it. That was the main concept I came away with.

I also came away knowing with every fibre of my being that property was my ticket to freedom.

Nobody offered property support and mentoring in those days, and even if they had I could never have afforded it. But having done the religious thing for years I was quite comfortable talking to anybody, so every time I saw builders working on a house, I'd pop in and ask them questions. I'd ask things like, "What are you doing?", "How much did you pay for that?", "What's the owner doing?", "Why are you doing it that way or this way?" I would just talk to everybody in my neighborhood about what they were up to. I learned what was selling, why it was selling, how it was selling, how long it was taking to sell—everything.

The problem now was that I had no money.

So after about six months on benefits, I got a full-time job as a trainer. I hated it. I'd never trained anybody in my life, but because I was chatty and confident, they trained me up for the job. Sometimes we have to do things we may not like or enjoy in order to get where we need to go, so I buckled down. Finally, I was able to start saving and get off benefits.

That job was the step I needed. I continued being as frugal as if I were still on benefits, which allowed me to start saving up for a deposit on a house. I didn't yet know all the creative ways to raise money that I know now, so it took another year or so before I could even get started.

Because I'd learned so much from going around talking to everybody, by then I knew all about the buy-to-let strategy. I knew that I could buy with the bank, do the house up, refinance, and borrow all my money back. So that's what I did, and it absolutely scared me to death when I took on the debt.

I remember often thinking, "Oh no, what am I doing?" I would have nightmares all the time about losing the house. But despite those fears and being stretched way outside of my comfort zone, I realised after six months that it was working.

My big moment was when the rent came into the bank account that first month. I didn't really believe it at first; I think it took six months for me to believe that it was really going to keep coming in.

After your first property, you get better and it gets easier. You learn new strategies and ways to adapt. Eventually I was able to draw a little extra cash out of each property so I could do two at a time, and then four at a time, and at one point my daughter and I were doing ten at a time when she came to work with me. The momentum grows and grows once you've taken that first step.

We always think of our first property as the toughest, but then you come out the other side and you're able to do six, eight, or ten at a time with ease.

I got more proficient at what I was doing and my relationship with the bank grew; they were giving me a lot of money. Eventually they stopped coming out to value the properties; they just conducted an evaluation and within a few days the money was in my bank. Within 10 days I'd bought the house, and within four weeks the project was done and I had my money back. We were receiving that return and going through that cycle every eight weeks or so. It took me a year to get my first property, and it was another eight or nine months before the second, but those first projects gave me feedback that my efforts were working and it just grew from there.

I think we need that sort of feedback to keep on going. People often think the biggest obstacle is not knowing what to do, or getting money together, or learning the market. But for me, the biggest challenges were always in my head, all internal. I was brought up with no feedback on anything I achieved, because all our achievements were religious-based. I talk about this with my clients, because it's these challenges that will hold us back, not the market and not the money.

I didn't think I was clever enough. I hadn't gained any O-levels and I held no degrees. I didn't think I was important enough to be able to do something significant. I thought, "I'm a woman, so therefore I'm the wrong gender".

I didn't believe I fitted into the property world.

The men were all big and had loud voices. I even felt I wasn't tall enough to be successful; I suppose I was intimidated by the stature of successful people.

I also had a lot of limited thinking about money! I thought it was wrong to be wealthy. I had been taught, "Wealthy people are evil, and if they have wealth, they must have stepped on someone to get there. They don't look after their families as they're working too hard for their money to live their values."

It was all these internal things that blocked me.

One of my biggest internal blocks came from being raised in an environment where we always had "just enough." My mum would say, "We've got just enough to cover that." I remember replacing the top step of the carpet on the stairs, because the top step always seemed to go threadbare, because it was "just enough" to keep that carpet for another few years.

With my new-found belief that this new business was going to work, it was now time to create financial stability: I didn't want to work full-time forever.

No challenge was going to stop me at this point, even if I sat in bed crying at night (which I did many times), I composed myself and kept on going.

Once I was working on a house that was just a little rental, and I would always go to see if the builders were happy. One day, the decorator who I was chatting with said to me, "Why aren't you doing this like Fred is?"

I asked him, "Oh, what's Fred doing?" and he told me Fred was making all the rooms into bedrooms and then putting in refugees and charging weekly rent.

I got in my car and went to Fred's office, not knowing if he would talk to me or not. I had only three properties by then, but Fred, a real Northern guy, liked that I was trying so hard and took me under his wing for a few months.

He advised me what to do: we changed the house layout, got all the contracts with the government, and then tenanted them.

These changes quadrupled my rent on that one little house, so I did it over and over.

Sometimes people come into your life for a reason to give you a gift, a lesson, or both.

I never had a direct mentor. The main people I saw in the industry were aggressive males. It was always about doing things to get the opponents out the way; I wasn't like that and didn't want to be. I had to do business my way, which is gentle, friendly, and chatty. It's win-win because I need to know that they're happy and I'm happy.

Within two years, I had given up the day job because I had enough rental income to support me and to employ my oldest daughter. Within two years I was what they call "financially free". I had my time back.

Those two years seemed like a long time because I was working full-time, doing property stuff on Saturdays, and having family time on Sundays, but it was so worth it. My girls were my drive; they were my big reason WHY, and spending at least some downtime with them every week was very important to me.

I firmly believe in the mind-body connection and always make sure I'm aligned with something I want to do. In fact, I think making sure that I love what I do has helped me immensely. The day I don't love something, I'll stop doing it. But I love property and that's what saw me through the long journey to get things set up properly.

Now that we had all these rents coming in, I felt secure enough to grow the business. I think we must have done upwards of 500 properties, and we kept many of them and the rest we sold. My pot of capital was getting bigger as was my rental income, and more importantly my experience, skills, and self-belief were growing.

In the beginning, it seemed strange—I would earn a bulk of money, but then trust the wrong people. Even though my intuition would tell me, "Don't do this, Belinda", I'd do it anyway and lose the money.

Then I'd have to start again. After I did that twice, I had to examine and work on that internal belief, because I realised it was something inside me that was making me sabotage myself.

Remember, I had a belief of having "just enough".

I did a lot of work around accepting that I deserved wealth and getting clear on what I would do next time this feeling came up for me—and it wasn'tt long before I had the opportunity to put myself to the test.

The next time I made a lump sum of money I was prepared. I thought, "Right, okay, this belief is going to come up again. How am I going to manage this? This time I am going to believe that I can take care of this money. I know what to do and I am going to keep it safe, and I can have more than enough."

I found that as soon as I had more money, somebody would show up in my life with a great thing that could earn money—and of course they always told me it was going to be easy. When that happened, I would remember the promise to myself: "I'm going to take care of this; I know how to look after this."

Every time a challenge came up, emotional or mental, I would examine it and try to put a better belief inside. It takes practise to become good at installing a better belief system, but once you find a new belief you will not accept the old belief anymore.

I had learned my lesson and chosen more empowering beliefs.

Now, if somebody shows up with a tempting offer that isn't aligned, I'm able to brush it aside without even a thought.

The biggest challenges are always internal. They are about believing in yourself. Believing you deserve it. And it's so worth believing you do, getting started, and staying the course!

I now have the privilege of living between Barbados, Spain, and the UK. Not for the sunbathing (though I do love the sunshine), but for the freedom of getting up, sitting outside, having a coffee, listening to the sea, swimming in the ocean, and feeling alive.

My family can visit and we can spend time together. In the morning, because I'm five hours behind the UK, I get up and do about two or three hours of work: just progressing things and trying to add value to my property deals or my clients that are on their own property journeys.

My family assists in taking care of the business as they are now part of the legacy of financial freedom. They take care of my multi-million-pound deals. They go out to assess the deals, do all the paperwork, go to viewings, and attend meetings. I chat with them every day and we progress deals together.

I always make sure to eat healthily. I realise, having been burnt out before, how important it is to put some me time in there, so I always make sure to quiet my busy mind and try to go to yoga three times a week. I try to take a nice long walk on the beach, probably around teatime when it's a little bit cooler.

The rest of my time is spent meeting up with friends and family three or four times a week for lunch. I make sure to go out every week dancing with friends as it makes me feel alive and young. As a family we plan trips together and go on spa days. What we work for is to create memories, and I make sure we do that. We are a very close family.

I just got back off holiday with my sister. We went away for ten days. There are only five years between my sister and me. We went to San Pedro in Spain for ten days because we wanted to find a home there to buy. I planned to rent first, then buy land and build.

When we got there, we went out the first night at 10 o'clock dancing, socialising, and chatting with people. We got back in the early hours of the morning; we were just going with the flow.

In ten days of being in Marbella, we never got to see one rental or one piece of land, and we just laughed about it. We did meet a fantastic real estate agent in a restaurant. He has been emailing me properties since the trip. He knows the area well and we are going to see where that goes. So in the end, the trip gave me what I needed without having to work on it, while my sister and I just had a good time.

I like to think I'm in the flow of life today. I know I must keep my energy flowing for everything else to work. I do realise now the importance of my role in the larger operation of what is called "my life". It's not about how many properties I own or remodel, it's about creating an energy flow within our environment—because then things just work with ease and grace.

After I had built up property with an income that would come in every month, and has for over 20 years now, I was secure in knowing I could meet all my and my family's needs. I then started to buy and sell. We started with small property flips, and then I got creative in securing properties, sometimes without even buying them. I would put planning on them and sell them on for hundreds of thousands of pounds in profits. I also would secure large pieces of land with contracts and get planning, and then sell them on for large profits or even develop them myself.

I have done title splits, HMO leases, bought and sold industrial units, bought land and split, and done large commercial deals with apartments and retail spaces.

I then decided to go into new builds and, instead of doings four or five houses, I did 22 homes in my first new-build development. We did the deal from beginning to end: we found the land, got the planning, secured a building company, and built the 22 homes. We still own these and rent them out for further cash flow, and we named them after my grandsons. They are very proud of that. When you make decisions with your own money, little by little you build confidence to take bigger and faster action. We were in a flow of what worked and I knew we could now create any win-win deal and profits in any market condition with property. That in itself gives you a calmness of mind and knowledge that you will always be financially secure.

We gained momentum over the years as I was very creative in doing deals with no money or very little money, and doing joint ventures with others such that it was a win-win for all concerned. I made sure everyone was happy with the deal and things went smoothly. Again, I was putting my own energy into my business and this flowed into the people we were dealing with and who we attracted to do business with. I proved you could do business whilst still being gentle, friendly, and honest. It is a myth that you have to be aggressive and cutthroat to get ahead.

Another belief I had changed. In fact, I know I have changed so many of my beliefs over the years that I am not the same person, and have a lot fewer beliefs that limit me. I changed what I believe about money, how much a woman can create, how much I am worth, what I could do, and how much time, money, and freedom I could create. Even today I know if I hit a hurdle, there is a belief to be examined. I know we must change our beliefs on the inside, if anything is to change on the outside.

Today, we do fewer deals. We only do multi-million-pound deals as it was my goal to work smarter each year. Remember I wanted time freedom along with an income; I never had the money as a goal. The money has come as a huge bonus to adding value to others. We normally do new builds or refurbishments where we buy old office blocks and do from 50 to 100 apartments at a time, or build new homes and care homes.

When you grow both internally and externally, you create a wave that also carries others. From my journey, my girls have gone on to create their own lettings agency and invest in property. So has my grandson who at the age of 18 got onto the property ladder and now knows how to evaluate multi-million pound deals that we invest in as a company. Whilst this is our life now, I still remember my first goal to just earn an extra £50 per week. A goal so small now, but back then it was a goal that meant I had enough each week. Baby steps can create a journey to freedom.

After five years I had created a lifestyle where I spent six months in the UK and six months traveling the world, and had the privilege of spending long stretches of time in Cape Town. In fact, I even went on to get four bungalows on a lease contract, and then got planning for 44 apartments that were then sold to a developer. The fundamental principles of good property investing and trading you can take anywhere in the world.

Oops, going off track again...

I enjoyed travelling all around South Africa, which I loved so much that for nine years straight I went back for six months a year. I travelled Greece, Spain, Italy, and most of the Caribbean Islands.

I then fell in love with the Caribbean and have been there for almost seven years now—who would have thought, from where I started and needing £50, this would be what I had created and achieved. Not a day goes by that I do not give thanks for it.

I believe that the universe sends you subtle whispers. Subtle whispers that get louder with time—you know the ones. *You are in the wrong job, in the wrong country, with the wrong person, in the wrong environment.* I believe it is our job to listen and then take action, no matter how small the steps are towards those desires that are coming from our soul.

At the same time, we must appreciate what we have and where we are now.

An example of this is that every night I would light a vanilla candle and give thanks for what I had, the air we breathed, my two girls, the roof over our heads, and that I had the opportunity to work on myself even if I had very little time.

One thing I reflect on in my journey as this brought me into a good space: nothing had changed but my inner being was at peace. I remember I would buy second-hand clothes from the market. The lady went and bought these from high-class people, and I got to wear tailored clothes for pennies, so I always felt wealthy. Every Friday I would go into a posh hotel and sit and have a coffee and a glass of water as then I could sit there longer to enjoy the feeling of wealth: this made me feel good, therefore attracting more good feelings to me.

No matter how bad things got, I worked on feeling grateful and wealthy.

I went on to create lots of little rituals that helped me stay on my journey and stay focused and feeling good. I later realised all this is called my "mindset".

I believe you have your own goals and the universe has other plans, and this certainly has proven true for me.

One day whilst I was in Barbados, I got a phone call from a friend who was in tears—real sobbing, heartfelt tears. My first thought was someone had died. My friend went on to explain through gasps of tears that at the age of 58 and two years away from retiring, the pension company she had invested into all her life had gone bust as they had mismanaged all the funds.

Then she asked me what became a life-changing question that altered the course of my life:

"Belinda, if you lost everything and had no money and no credit, what would you do?"

In an instant, I knew within a year I could create wealth and be back in Barbados in my home on the beach. It was only in that moment that I realised how valuable my life, journey, experience, and knowledge were...

How could I not share this with others?

This was never a thought of mine, but the universe had sent me a powerful signal—was I going to follow it?

I felt I had no choice. Another fire was lit in my belly – to help others create financial freedom and enjoy a life they aspire to so they can live their lives to the full.

There was no going back...

You see, I believe a mentor has to have done what they are teaching you to do, and proved they can take you on the same journey and know all aspects of not only the outside journey (buying, financing, raising money, doing deals with no money, etc.) but can help you with what will be the toughest part of the journey: the internal side, your own limiting beliefs, your fears of not being good enough, clever enough, knowledgeable enough, deserving enough, your fear of talking to a lawyer, a bank manager, or an investor. You might laugh, but, as I mentioned earlier, one of my worries was that I was not tall enough to be successful.

The mindset is where I get to really help my clients: where I can cut out all the rubbish and noise around property and get straight to the heart of creating financial freedom.

Today I share my property strategies for helping others with my team of mentors and coaches, so together we can deliver real strategies that work in today's market, whilst building confidence and self-worth and getting rid of those limiting self-beliefs.

I am often asked what I am most proud of and it is not the money. It is the emotional wins that I feel overwhelmed and privileged to have achieved.

I took on my dad as our Property Maintenance Manager after he worked all his life in factories. He absolutely loved driving around in his little white van and taking care of all our family properties. He knew the tenants by name. They all loved him and many would cook for him. He spent six years with me before he retired.

In that time, I saw my dad blossom into a very happy man who loved going to work...

Priceless.

Sometimes things get you when you're not expecting them. When my mum told me my dad was going to take a loan out for a car at 74 years of age, I was so upset. I told them to go find a car and I would pay for it. To be able to give is such an incredible feeling and even just relaying the story makes me cry. All of this was possible because I took action and had a big WHY.

My mum and dad came from a generation that did not talk about money. One day I pushed my mum to tell me how they were financially, and she said she was, "keeping her head above water." That struck me as a very difficult situation, and not one I wanted my parents to be in. So I said, "Finish your tea Mum. We are going to set something up."

We walked over to the bank and I deposited some money into her account to give my parents a cushion, and told her how much I would put in at the end of every single month so she did not have to worry about money anymore. She broke down in tears in the bank and said she was so relieved as it had been keeping her awake at night. For this opportunity, I am immensely thankful and it still brings me to tears.

Until recently, I had never heard my mum say, "I'm waiting for the spring collection of a clothes line." It fills my heart with joy to hear of her purchases and holidays after being so frugal all her life.

I am filled with... How can you describe feelings of joy? I am overwhelmed and emotional to see my own girls grow into fine young women who I know are financially better off than most. They know they can create time and freedom with money in their own lives and now the lives of their children, too. Their mind-sets have changed into what they believe a woman, and indeed their children, can achieve.

It is a legacy that will continue for generations. Wow. Who would have thought someone like me could set all this in motion?

I'm very proud that we work together as a family: my girls, their partners, my brother-in-law, my grandson, my nephew—all working together in the property industry and property educational training industry.

I mentioned earlier that my first grandson, who did his apprenticeship with me, got his first home at the age of 18. He understands how to use his money and other people's money to create assets.

I am proud that property has gone beyond me to others that have worked for me and are now on their own journeys, and that they have included their families. We never know what a chain reaction we can create that impacts so many lives. I feel blessed to see how the property training has changed so many other women's and their partners' lives to create a better standard of living, a chance to be in better schools, and the ability to give back to the community with their heart-centred donations and skills.

I now believe without a question of doubt no matter what comes up, you can get over it. Because I know there is nothing you can't get over—the divorce, the separation, the religion, not having enough money, lack of a formal education, time constraints, bad credit, no friends. Nothing. How do I know? I know because I had a burning WHY, which was to be a great example to my girls, and none of the above stopped me. Therefore, if you want a change there is nothing that will stop you.

This is the space I hold for my clients... I believe they can do this...

My business has allowed me to enjoy everything I ever wanted. It's given me the time and freedom to make memories with my family and friends.

That is the prize: making memories and enjoying feeling alive in exactly the way YOU want.

I have been asked if there was a set of events that shaped me, and as I look back there have been many. However, the significant ones that catapulted my journey were the three single most important factors that kept me on track, motivated, and determined not to quit. I feel humbled and honoured to share these with you, and I hope you can find the things that will shape your journey for the future.

First, it all started with an ABSOLUTE DECISION. Let me explain.

I was at that point of not having enough money and sitting on the rented lounge floor crying, not knowing a way out and feeling helpless, useless, and hopeless. I looked up at the universe (I did not like God at this stage) and cried out:

"This is not how I want to live and is not the example I want for my girls. It has to change! Show me a way."

I promised no matter how uncomfortable, scared, fearful, or intimidated I was, I would not stop. It was a decision I knew I would never go back on—it was absolute!

Two weeks later I saw that advert in the local paper on property training and creating time, money, and freedom.

It was my sign! I had to act!

Second, I always connected to my big WHY. You see, my reason for all this was bigger than earning a little extra money, or buying a bag or a new car: it was being the greatest example of a mother, woman and provider that I could be to my girls, and to show them what was possible. So, no matter how tired I was, no matter how fearful I was, no matter what I did not know, or how slow things seemed to go, I would NEVER quit. The WHY was bigger than all my fears and all my excuses.

Your big WHY—that goal that gets you out of bed when you feel helpless, makes you make that telephone call whilst feeling sick with fear, helps you sleep on a restless night when you think you are totally out your depth—it is the driving inner force that never sleeps and never lets up.

Third, the next significant step that kept me and my mind on track and still does, is that I always kept my mind, body, and soul in a good space (well, almost always—no one is perfect).

This is what they call "gratitude" today. I just called it, "giving thanks."

Every night, even to this day nearly 20 years on, I light a French vanilla candle, as I just love the scent and it calms me, and I give thanks for the day, the people, the signs, and the feelings I had that day.

Even when I had no money, I gave thanks that I saw others with money and that mine was on its way. I gave thanks for all the wonderful variety in the shops as I knew these were available to me. I gave thanks I had love and could give love, and I gave thanks no matter how slow I was on my journey to financial freedom. This ritual allowed me to go to bed in a calm, thankful, and receptive mood—and that is how I would wake up.

I know that getting into a space of thankfulness for what we have opens the door to receive more into our lives.

I have taught my grandchildren to go to bed each evening and say five things they are thankful for, and this leaves them in a good space to snuggle and go to sleep.

The next message I want to leave loud and clear is this. Start exactly where you are.

No money? Start.
No education? Start.

Don't know what to do? Start.

In debt? Start.

On welfare? Start.

Find someone that inspires you and follow them, and lastly, never, ever quit.

Make that absolute decision, find your big WHY, and be thankful.

I am blessed to share my story and my hope is that it has lit a fire in your belly to create the life of your dreams, because I am living proof no matter where you start from, IT IS POSSIBLE!

Big Hugs xxx

KEVIN PONESKIS

I decided I was going to leave the Army, but I
wanted to leave without the need to get a job

Kevin Poneskis has been investing in property since 1991. He also
served for 24 years in the British Army serving in a Commando
Regiment. He left the Army in 2011 without the need to get a job
because of his investing in property. He now has a multi-million
pound portfolio of single-lets and HMOs and Serviced
Accommodation units.

Business: Property Investor, Trainer and Mentor

Services offered: Property Training and Mentoring

Email: info@propertysoldier.co.uk

Website: www.propertysoldier.co.uk

*

Before I started in property around the age of 20, I was the son of a soldier. My father met my mum in Plymouth when he was in 29 Commando Regiment RA in Plymouth. He'd actually previously been in the SAS, so as you can imagine, he was quite imposing. He was someone I always looked up to, and I still do, having always tried to follow in his footsteps. I'm one of four kids, twelve in total, as he has been married three times – although he had four kids with my mum Kathy who was his second wife. I followed him around with my siblings to different locations in the UK and Germany, as kids in the forces will do; I was a 'Squaddy brat' if you will. I went to around 20 different schools throughout my childhood in Germany and the UK. My dad would be getting posted all over the place and on very short notice would be told, "You need to go there now" and we would follow. In order to try to slow down this changing of schools, a lot of families in the forces put their kids into boarding schools so that the parents can move around with the military and the kids can stay in one place.

At age nine, I went to boarding school but unfortunately that didn't last too long because I was expelled at age ten – that was quite an interesting time. I can remember things like getting caned, getting pulled by the hair, and having my head banged off the table at dinner. At one point, I was taken to the doctor's because the marks on my backside from being caned weren't healing and they'd become infected.

I'd always been quite the rebellious kid, so I used to be a bit cheeky and naughty and the headmaster would administer punishment as he saw fit. That same rebellious streak in me caused me to not be willing to accept this treatment, and I actually ran away from school and stayed out over a weekend, which caused a bit of commotion and a police search for me. I had walked off in the direction of the cliffs – this is in Tynmouth, in Devon – and I walked at night along the coastal cliff path in the direction of Dawlish Warren, where I found a barn to sleep in. I had raided the pantry in the boarding house to get some food before going on my escape and evasion exercise, and when I had decided I was cold, hungry and dishevelled enough, I headed back in the direction of the school and was picked up by a police car which took me back to the school. I was put in a room where I was given lines to write: "I must not run away," or something like that. I wrote hundreds and hundreds of lines until my uncle who lived in Plymouth arrived to take me away from the school: I had been expelled.

Not long after that the school closed down for various reasons. I don't know whether I was the catalyst for that, but I'd like to think I had some part to play in stopping the behaviour. That was one of the many schools I attended during my childhood. I ended up going to another boarding school after that – I'm not trying to say all boarding schools are bad because they certainly aren't.

The next boarding school I went to was also in Devon, the Queen Elizabeth school in Crediton, and I was there for a couple of years, and it was a really good experience that I enjoyed a lot. I went to several schools, but knew I wanted to join the army because of my father, so as soon as I could leave school at age 16 I did.

My dad had been quite famous in the army; he was a very successful soldier. My very first day in the army, this scary Scotsman called Sergeant Hogg was calling out the nominal roll and everyone was answering to their name. He read out my name and stopped dead in his tracks, asking in his very strong Scottish accent, "Who's Poneskis?" and quivering, I said, "Me, Sergeant." He said, "Was your old man Jock Poneskis?" I said, "Yes, Sergeant." He said, "Poneskis, your old man used to give me fuck all. Now I'm going to give you fuck all." From that day on, I got really good at doing press-ups! I still do them every single day; I'm very good at press-ups so it didn't do me any harm. I actually quite enjoyed being in the army. I joined the military because my dad was in the army, not because it was "in my blood" or anything like that. I now know that I'm more of an entrepreneur than a soldier, but people continue to have this perception of me: "Oh you did 24 years in the army; you must be naturally organised and efficient." I'm actually the same as most people on that front, I've just had to work hard at it.

I went from "boy service," as they call it, into the adult army. Meanwhile my dad, having left the army, got into property and started buying houses. Because I followed in my dad's footsteps, when he suggested that I also invest in property, I did. I bought a little flat in Plymouth in 1991 and rented it out, and still have it today. I bought that for £30,000 and when I could afford to buy another, bought one just opposite on the same street. I bought that for £22,000, because the market was on its way down at the time in the early 1990s. I still have it, and although the market was on its way down, it's now worth in excess of £100,000, and the other one is similar. One of my mantras now, having been a property investor for such a long time and not having sold during the recessions, is: "Don't wait to buy property; buy property and wait."

My dad convinced me that it was a good idea, and because I'm entrepreneurial I didn't take much convincing. I'd seen him do pretty well out of it, although he was buying properties in the 1980s when the market was on the up. So a lot of the success was due to general market appreciation at the time. When I started buying, the market was on the way down. It hit the bottom in the mid 1990s and then climbed significantly. Even though the mortgage interest rates got to 15%, my rents were still covering the mortgages. By the mid 1990s, I had a house in Swansea that my dad sourced and let out for me, and two flats in Plymouth which I managed and let out personally. At the time, I didn't actually know much about the fact that the houses were depreciating in value. I wasn't a trained or knowledgeable property investor and was pretty much just flying by the seat of my pants. In retrospect, it all turned out to be okay because property can be very forgiving, and if you can hold onto it for long enough, the values tend to sort themselves out with long-term appreciation. I think a lot of people lose money when they sell because of a recession. If you keep hold of it, it will likely recover and return a handsome profit over time. That's a lesson that I've learned in property having now been an investor through two recessions.

After joining up, I was in the 'Field Army' as it was called, until 1995 based mainly on Salisbury Plain in the Royal Artillery. Then aged 25, I applied to go to 29 Commando Regiment in Plymouth and I successfully passed the Commando Course and was awarded my Green Beret, of which I am immensely proud. My next purchase was a large property that used to be a guesthouse, which I bought in 2005. It was on the Hoe in Plymouth, and I moved into it with my then wife and split the property, making a self-contained flat downstairs where my wife and I lived, and four rooms upstairs that I let out.

I found being a property investor okay until I started to get deployed overseas on operations. That's when things became complicated, because ultimately I found myself juggling too many balls at once, and it became an extremely stressful thing to do because I didn't have the right systems in place that a property investor should have in order to grow a portfolio and have a full-time job.

Before I went to 29 Commando at age 22, I had been in a relationship with a lady and we had a daughter called Siân, but with the help of my mum I decided I wanted to apply for custody. In the end, the social workers supported our application as a result of their own investigation into Siân's wellbeing. We won the custody case and with the help of my mum and my family we brought Sian up from the age of six months, and this is how things were until Siân was nine years old. It was at this time that I met my first wife. We met and got married really quickly and Siân moved in with us. Unfortunately the marriage was a mistake and it didn't last one year. When I returned from an Army deployment my wife told me that she was with someone else and she wanted a divorce. I had to load all of Siân's and my own things into my car and leave. It was not a very pleasant time.

I had to act very quickly to get Siân into a new school in time for the next term and so I managed to get her into a really good boarding school in Plymouth called Plymouth College. My Army camp was only 5 minutes away and my Mum was also just around the corner and so it worked really well. If things didn't work out, I always had the option to leave the Army and live with Siân full time, but I decided to try this solution for the time being. It turned out that Siân, now aged 11, loved it at Plymouth College and she thrived there, whilst at the same time she had very regular access to me and my family. We would even meet up for lunch and in the evenings, which is very different to most people's experience of boarding school.

Sian was in her teens when I got married again. My second wife, who I was with for about five years, got on really well with Siân. But she didn't really want to have that sort of family-type situation so Siân stayed in the boarding school. To be fair, Siân was very happy there. We were living in Plymouth and the boarding school was only a few minutes away. Quite often, because she was thriving and loving boarding life so much, she would actually stand us up and say, "Do you mind if I do this school activity instead? I want to do this with the other kids." She was very happy at the school and we were very close by, so it turned out to be fine.

Siân stayed on at Plymouth College right through to completing her A Levels and went on to Nottingham University, graduating in 2015, and is now fluent in French, German and Spanish and at the time of writing living in Saint-Malo, France. She's an international recruitment consultant and is extremely happy with her life. Though it's been a struggle, I'm very glad I applied for custody of Siân and did not decide to leave her with her mother, but I could not have done it without the help of my mum, my family, and my second wife.

When I was deploying and going overseas, my second wife was very supportive with Siân and was the shoulder to cry on that a teenage girl needs. Siân and my second wife are still quite close, and Sian still talks and meets with her. It's all turned out for the best, but was very difficult at times.

One of those stressful times was my first tour to the Balkans, in Kosovo during the Balkans war, where there was essentially ethnic cleansing going on, with the fighting between the Serbs, Croats and the Albanians. That was a six-month operation and obviously when things like that start happening, it's difficult to manage a property portfolio, maintain your personal relationships, and bring up your daughter at the same time.

I had a property portfolio but no proper systems in place, so I was managing it myself with no letting agents. I was putting tenants in without credit referencing, and so would sometimes have tenant issues and voids (periods without a tenant) which was hard to deal with at times.

I suppose I made life a bit harder for myself because I then applied to join the SAS and had two attempts at getting in – my dad was in the SAS, so there's a pattern there! My knees were causing me a lot of trouble and I had to get Cortisone injections directly into the knee joints to try to alleviate the pain. My knee problems prevented me from actually getting to the point at which they might have said yes or no to me and so I have no idea whether I would have got in if I hadn't been injured. Trying to get in the SAS just complicated things further in terms of extra things to juggle.

Shortly afterwards I came very, very close to going to Iraq – I was literally about to go the next day, but then my Regiment decided to keep me in the UK and swap who they were sending. The reason for this was I was on loan to a different Regiment at the time, who were not deploying to Afghanistan, and they fought to keep me which stopped me from going, which created mixed emotions for me at the time.

Several of my friends from the 29 Commando were killed on that tour of Iraq, which was tragic. I had to carry one of their coffins draped in the Union flag at his funeral and later help to lower him into the ground. My friend was called Llewelyn Evans and he was from Llandudno in North Wales. That's the hardest thing I have ever done, but insignificant compared to the hardship and grief suffered by his family.

Although I didn't go to Iraq, I later deployed to Afghanistan twice. Prior to going to Afghanistan for the first time, a friend of mine, Jim, went with a different Regiment. Tragically Jim was killed. Just after attending his funeral, I deployed for the first time. He'd been killed in a place called Forward Operating Base Robinson, and that's where I was sent first, which was just a surreal and very unnerving situation. During that tour, four men from 29 Commando were killed. I knew them all well. Indeed one of the guys, called Mick, was the same rank as me and we shared a tent from time to time in Camp Bastion. On this occasion I wasn't able to attend the funerals back home, but we had to carry the coffins on to the airplane draped in the Union flag and say our goodbyes there and then.

Life just seemed to get more and more complicated. I was now trying to manage a portfolio of property from a war zone and I was having to rely more and more on my wife back home who was in a full-time job herself. We were having tenant problems, which was really stressful and causing a strain on the marriage. The tour did not start well, because I was just about to get on the plane to go when she phoned me up in an awful state because of a massive flood at our house on the Hoe, caused by the gutters being blocked from rainwater pouring in off three large roofs that drained onto ours. The rainwater was supposed to drain through a pipe that went through the loft and out, but the pipe blocked and instead hundreds, if not thousands, of gallons of water just started pouring down into the three-storey house. That's why she was calling me saying, "Help!" It was awful because I could do very little to help her. I got to the other end and I still couldn't phone until I was eventually able to get hold of the satellite phone to speak to a very fed up wife and to ask how things were now in the house that had just been ruined.

Things like that were a challenge, and after my second tour of Afghanistan where we lost another two men from 29 Commando, I got back and she asked for a divorce. We divorced amicably; there was no one else involved. It had just run its course and she didn't want to be married any more. In order to give a divorce settlement, I agreed to sell four of the houses. We had bought a very nice, fancy, waterside apartment with floor-to-ceiling windows looking out over Plymouth Sound. Ultimately it wasn't the best decision in the world in terms of being an investment property, but I put that on the market to sell, and also put three of the flats on the market in order to give her a divorce settlement. At that time – this was 2010 – we were in the height of the recession and nothing was selling for the price I needed it to in order to give her a divorce settlement. Unfortunately, I moved tenants out and spent a lot of money refurbishing to sell them, but then my debt started racking up and up, because I was getting no rent and paying all the bills and they weren't selling. I got myself into quite a sticky situation financially and was getting quite desperate.

I was now a Regimental Sergeant Major, so I had been promoted up through the ranks to the highest rank you can reach as a soldier, and was posted away from Plymouth to Luton. I was going through a divorce and it was then that I met Caroline, who I'm still with today. At the time Caroline didn't know I was in a tricky financial situation or have any idea how hard being with a soldier is long-term because I was in a pretty stable role which didn't require me to go away much.

At this time, Caroline received two free tickets from her dad to go to a free property investing seminar. At that point I had been investing in property for 20 years, but I didn't yet know what was possible with property. So we went on this seminar, which actually completely opened my eyes to what I could go on to achieve, and I signed up for some training. My outlook on life completely changed at this point because I believed that by implementing the strategies that I was now being taught, I could become financially free through property.

I knew I had to make a change because at that time I was actually trapped in a job because of my property, since I was using my employment income to pay for my portfolio which was on the whole taking money out of my pocket because I had either bought the wrong type of property or I wasn't operating it properly. I didn't know how to be a proper property investor, so to speak. I had another Afghanistan tour looming and I really feared for my relationship with Caroline, worrying that our relationship wouldn't survive it. I was pretty desperate.

I signed up to all the training I could which got me in to more debt, but I knew that what I was learning would enable me to get myself out of debt and into profit a lot quicker than without the knowledge. One of the phrases I now love and use is: "If you want something different, you're going to have to do something different." In other words: if you always do what you've always done, you're always going to get what you always got.

It was at that point that I decided I was going to leave the Army, but I wanted to leave without the need to get a job and so I would have to make property investing work! From handing in my notice I would need to serve one full year before leaving, and so I would have a year to turn everything around if I was to achieve my goal. I knew when I handed it in that I wouldn't be able to take it back, because at the time they were shrinking the Army numbers and I had been warned that once you gave notice, you were out. I handed in my notice on Remembrance Day 2010, and left a year later on 11/11/11. I actually had a Colonel phoning me up saying, "What on earth are you doing? I know you're not supposed to be able to remove this or make this go away, but if you ask me to, I will hide your resignation and get rid of it for you. You've got a job for life. Think of your pension man." He and others were trying to talk me out of it and that was really hard for me because having done a lot of military parachuting during my career, I thought that I had essentially 'jumped out of the aircraft' and therefore couldn't decide to get back in! They made it really hard for me to stick to my guns and to say no; they were trying to talk me out of it and I just had to insist, because ultimately they were completely unqualified to give me financial advice. I am very pleased to say that during the next year I doubled my portfolio that until that point had taken me 20 years to build, but now my whole portfolio was putting good money into my pocket instead of taking money out and I indeed left the Army on 11/11/11 without the need to get a job. I chose Remembrance Day to leave the Army because it is a significant day for me and when I had made my mind up to leave the previous month, it just felt right to do it then. RIP lads, lest we forget.

47

Once Caroline and I embarked on the training we soon realised that in order to be successful it was going to take a lot more effort than just attending the courses! Unfortunately for a while we would get really excited during the training and fully intend to go on to implement everything we were being taught , but then we would go back to our jobs and back to our problems. I still had a daughter to bring up; she was a teenager and needed my time and support. I was still trying to sort out my divorce settlement: I had to let the properties back out because they weren't selling, and then I had to borrow a hell of a lot more money to give to my ex-wife as a divorce settlement. My job as a Regimental Sergeant Major was giving me a lot of paperwork and admin to attend to as well as events and parades to organise. In the Army the higher up the ranks you go, instead of driving a tank, you find yourself driving a desk! I wasn't actually finding the time to implement the property strategies that I was being taught.

I knew I had to do something differently, and so I sought out a property mentor to hold me accountable. One of the things that a good mentor will do is be straight, and to tell you to do what you know you should be doing and what you've been taught to do. One of the things I knew I should do at the time was to put an advert in the newspaper and get leaflets out, essentially trying to go direct to vendor (owner), and to get the vendors to invite you to make an offer on their property. My mentor told me that was what I should do next. Caroline and I were going and sitting with him and being given that advice: to do what we knew we should do. We were seeing him once a month, and just before going to see him the following month, we still hadn't done it – we hadn't placed the advert in the newspaper. We still hadn't made leaflets. But I just couldn't go back to him again and look him in the eye and say, "I haven't done it." To be honest, it was only half an hour's work, we just had to turn off the bloody television in the evening for half an hour and stop procrastinating. So we did, and we went back to him and said, "Yep, we've got the advert in the newspaper and we've done the leaflets." We bought 15 houses over the next couple of years as a result.

This taught me the power of getting mentored and essentially having someone holding you accountable for implementing what you already know you should be doing. A mentor can sometimes initially train you and then move on to helping you implement. But often, a mentor is just telling you what you already know you should do. The power of that, I now know, is very important. We all procrastinate, and we just say we'll do it tomorrow, but if someone is holding you to it, it's harder to put it off, and you therefore get the benefit of the training. You're in less danger of wasting your money if you get someone to mentor you once you've actually done the training. The difficulty is that it's just more money – you spent your money on the training and now you need to spend more money to get a mentor. But the likelihood of success if you have a mentor is so much greater than if you don't, so you have to decide for yourself whether or not it's a good use of your money.

In terms of defining moments in my career, there was a whole series of things, one after the other, that came to me and made me decide to leave the Army to become a full-time property investor. I just knew that I had to make a change because I would have gone on the next Afghanistan tour and probably would have still been in the Army today. The next rank for me would have been that of Captain, and I may even have been a Major by now, who knows. I do know that I would have ended up putting my relationship with Caroline under the same stresses as my previous relationships, and that wasn't a risk I was willing to take.

I would have probably had to continue propping up my property portfolio with my job because of not being trained properly, and not having the correct systems in place. I was not properly vetting tenants and setting the tenancies up with the right methods of payment. I knew I had to do something different, because what I was doing was just not working. Getting some training was ultimately the big light that switched on for me and made me realise what was possible in property. It's not his fault but my dad had told me to invest in property – but he hadn't shown me how, and that was a problem, so I needed some proper training. The other thing is that you don't realise how much strain and pressure you're under until you actually see light at the end of the tunnel. You don't realise how hard life is until you're given a way out of the bind you're in.

One of the things I love to do, now that I'm full-time in property and can just focus on building my property portfolio, is actually help other people to be successful property investors , and to give then the chance to escape whatever hamster wheel they are on. Whatever it is they're doing to exchange their life or their time for money, because there is an alternative: they can create passive income from properties and have the choice to either work or not. Most people, once they build up their passive income from property to a certain level, actually choose not to work any more. Some people choose to carry on working part time.

Because I'm now a property trainer and mentor myself, one of the proudest things that I've done is convince my friend Harry to come to a free training event I was delivering. I encourage all my friends and family to get trained in property, but as they say, you can lead a horse to water but you can't make it drink. Harry had joined the Army a couple years after me; I was his best man and we were always good friends. Harry had left the Army and gone into security work like a lot of service men and women do after leaving the military. Unfortunately, in security, and especially in Harry's case, you spend more time away from family than when you are actually in the military. He had gone into maritime security and had been spending time on container ships, with their austere environments and lack of decent food and accommodation. He was just not enjoying life at all.

At the end of the free training events, you obviously have to pay if you would like further training. He didn't. I wasn't going to train him for free, because if something's free it feels like it doesn't have any value and you're less likely to take action and implement what you're taught. You should pay for the right training because it's a very valuable thing that you're going to learn from, and he didn't do it. He was staying with me and Caroline at our house that night, because he'd travelled down from near Nottingham and we were in Swansea. He kept asking me some more questions about the training that I'd done that day and I answered his questions but, after while, I said, "Look, Harry, do you want my advice?" He said, "Yeah." I closed his notebook because he was still taking notes. I said, "Give me your fu##ing credit card and get your ass on that training course that I advised you to go on earlier." He said "alright, alright calm down" and he gave me his card – we had a payment terminal – and we basically took his money for the training. I wasn't delivering the training that he was going to go on; I just knew that it was good training for him to attend. I texted him earlier in May this year to ask how he was doing, and as a result of the training, he's now got five properties and works part time in the reserve recruiting office because he enjoys just spending a bit of time being with people who are applying to join the army. He's always on holiday. He drives me crazy on Facebook with all the different countries he's visiting with his wife. He just said, "Thank you."

Today, while my business includes buying and selling property, and earning income from HMOs (houses of multiple occupation) and single lets, the main area of my work is serviced accommodation. People from all over the country and abroad will come and stay in our serviced accommodation units, which are apartments and houses that aren't anyone's primary residence. Ultimately, people will pay for a short stay ranging from one night up to just short of six months, which is our longest booking. The guests pay a per-night rate to stay in our accommodation, which is very similar to a hotel apart from the fact that they've got the whole house or apartment, kitchen, lounge etc. to themselves. When they arrive, there are towels on the bed, toiletries in the bathroom – everything is completely furnished and equipped with anything that they might possibly need. When our guests leave, the cleaners will go in and completely service it, changing all the bedding and towels, etc. for our next guests who will arrive. We are finding it to be a much better cash-flow strategy than our single lets and HMOs. Flipping property obviously gives you a lump sum, but it's not passive income. We're enjoying quite a significant income from our serviced accommodation units. While I still train people to build a portfolio, the best income-generating strategy to utilise and maximise the income from that portfolio is currently serviced accommodation, which does not involve having tenants, but you can always adapt and change course in this industry and so if a better strategy comes along I could always change to that one instead, although I think I will be doing serviced accommodation for a long time to come!

I am of the opinion that the serviced accommodation sector will continue to grow significantly and so there's a real opportunity for people to also get involved in it. Serviced Accommodation is what I mainly do and so it's therefore what I advocate other people do. The beauty of serviced accommodation is that you don't actually need to buy property in order to use serviced accommodation as an income-generating strategy. One of the things that we do is take other people's property and essentially act as a managing agent for that property using an agreement. This might be a property they may previously have been operating as a single let, for instance. We now use it as a serviced accommodation, and it's a complete win-win situation because we're able to handsomely reward the property owner from the income and earn a portion of the income ourselves for managing the property. One of the other things that we do is source property directly from letting agents and provide accommodation for our own corporate clients. For instance, we've just moved in a guest who works for Amazon, who travelled over from Barbados for a month – that booking was over £3,000 on a two-bed apartment. The monthly buy-to-let rent on the same apartment would be £650.

Because we require accommodation for our corporate clients, we will take properties from letting agents on a company-let agreement in order to service our corporate clients – it's another way in which you don't actually have to buy a property in order to generate income from serviced accommodation. It is simply a case of the agent asking the landlord or the owner of the property, "Are you happy to do a company let?" It's a very exciting strategy because there are multiple ways that you can source your properties in order to earn significant income from property. It's another string to the bow, if you will, in terms of single let, HMO, buying and selling, and serviced accommodation as the main strategies that we're implementing at the moment.

If somebody else wanted to start from scratch and achieve what I have, they would obviously need to get some training, because that's exactly what I needed in order to change the situation I had got myself into. As with anything, you clearly need to get the right training. There are multiple training providers out there – there are going to be some that are cheaper than others and there are going to be some that are better than others I would always advocate the necessity of getting a mentor to follow up and hold you accountable in addition to your training, because you're so much more likely to be successful as a result. I see the difference time and time again with people who get trained and mentored versus people who get trained and don't get mentored. That's ultimately what my advice would be to other people. I would never advise someone do something that I haven't personally done – that is one of my mantras.

There are a lot of good trainers and mentors out there; I like to think that I am one of the good ones. I've been investing in property for a very long time now and so I know how to do it wrong, but I also know how to do it right, so I can help people if they are struggling, because I've struggled. I have successfully helped people who have a lot on their plate because I've been in that position, too. Being a trainer and a mentor is not just about teaching the X, Y, Zs of property; it's ultimately about helping people overcome the challenges they're currently facing in life. If you have a lot of life experience yourself, then you're much more qualified and equipped to help other people. Ultimately, life is not easy, and one of the things I do tell people is to not look at a successful person and say to yourself, "It's alright for them, they don't have my challenges. They haven't got my problems." If you dig a little deeper, just about every successful person you will ever see will have overcome extreme hardship and challenges to get to where they are. What some people do is bury their head in the sand and say, "It's alright for them, they've obviously had things handed to them on a plate. They haven't got my challenges. They haven't got my problems." People give themselves the excuse of not even trying to have a go at changing their lot. The tragedy of it is that they're actually robbing themselves of the chance of achieving the success that they're capable of. My message is don't look at successful people and say, "It's alright for them, I couldn't do that."

I firmly believe that if you are honest with people and fair with them then you will be successful. To be successful as a property investor you do not have to exploit anyone, and you can create win-win situations. I'm very proud to say that as far as I'm concerned, in every single property deal I've done I have been honest about my offer, and whenever I can I will create a win-win situation for both the seller and myself.

In my experience, most people who are in a job are stressed, often don't have time to think about helping others, and certainly most people don't have the spare cash to think about helping others. Most people are just trying to keep their own head above water. It's an awesome situation to be in, when you actually find yourself to have more time and more money so that you can choose what you are going to do with your life, and who you are going to help.

One of the things that I enjoy doing now is helping a charity called STOLL that provides accommodation and support to homeless veterans. I was invited to meet the charity by a chap called Tom, who used to work for them. Unfortunately, he has just passed away, but he invited me to do an event in which people would pay money to listen to me speak about property, and the money raised would go to the charity. So, that got me introduced to the charity, and I've since done a few things like an abseil off the Broadgate Tower to raise some money for them. I've spoken at their annual Christmas Carol Service and met their patron, Sophie, Countess of Wessex, Prince Edward's wife.

I've also been inspired to write my own book, *Property Soldier*, in which I talk about my journey in the Army and the things I experienced as a soldier and as a property investor, and how I entered the property business full-time. Whilst I hope it is an interesting read, I also hope that it will provide some valuable information for people who are thinking about changing their lifestyle and getting into property investing. 100% of the profits of the book will go to the charity – my way of giving back to ex-servicemen and women who find themselves on hard times and who might not necessarily have had the opportunity to prepare themselves properly for leaving the military.

I feel very fortunate to have a lot more choice and freedom in my life now and it has been achieved by investing in property, but more importantly investing in my own education which has enabled me to become a successful property investor.

BINDAR DOSANJH

You don't have to be passionate about property; you have to be passionate about your life. Property is just a vehicle to get you there.

Business: Smart Core Wealth Ltd

Services offered: Property investment training and mentoring, and accountability coaching

Email: Info@smartcorewealth.com

Website: http://www.smartcorewealth.com/

*

We all have a story within us: we all have life-challenging moments and decisions to make throughout our lives and those are the ones that shape our destiny and make us the people we become.

I grew up in the late 1960s and early 1970s in Birmingham in England. My dad came to the UK in 1957 and my mum followed him in 1964. Both came with nothing from Punjab in North West India. Neither of them had any education and could not read or write but they were hard-working individuals. My childhood was a balancing act of my parents' imposing their upbringing on my siblings and I, their demands, their way of thinking versus the Western society. I came from a strict traditional Indian family, where women were brought up to be housewives while the men were the main breadwinners taking care of the family finances. This is what was expected of me which was fine, as my siblings and I knew no better.

We didn't have very much money when we were growing up. At times, we had second-hand outfits and Dad saved every penny so he could provide us with a better life. I remember the time we had to rent a VHS video recorder for the weekend because my parents couldn't afford to actually buy one outright. Dad was such a kind and generous man; he would help others with financial problems and give them money to buy their first home or business.

I went to a Catholic secondary school. There were only four Indian children at our school: two Indian girls and two Indian boys and we experienced racial bullying. We didn't have very many friends, as we were not allowed to socialise after school. We had to come home straight from school, do our homework and then help our mother in the kitchen with the household chores. I wasn't afraid of hard work: while I was growing up, to make some extra money, I did babysitting, was an Avon sales representative and had a newspaper round.

We weren't encouraged to stay on at school and going to university wasn't encouraged at all. However, I wanted to be a doctor and at school my older brother fought for me to do the three science subjects so I could have the right subjects to follow that line of work.

I soon realised that being a doctor wasn't for me when my dad had a nose bleed. I came to his rescue and, as soon as I saw my dad's blood all over the floor, I fainted. Thinking it was a one-off instance, I decided to support my younger brother and go with him to the dentist when he had his teeth extracted. I fainted again and there was a chain of other similar incidents. And so I discovered I couldn't stand blood and injections so I could never be a doctor or even a nurse. I went to see my school career's advisor who suggested I should become a medical secretary stating that I could "hang around with the doctors and nurses." I thought, "That's a great idea."

I got engaged on my eighteenth birthday. It was an arranged marriage. My parents' met my potential in-laws at our local temple. They both decided that my potential husband and I would be a good match and the families should be united. So, whilst I was waiting to get married at 20, I went to college to do a medical secretarial course. I was scared about my future married life in London, as I had never been to London. We didn't even often go into Birmingham city centre. The only reality I knew was school, home, work, the temple and visiting relatives. There was no travelling abroad or to other towns in the UK, so you could say I lived a settled life.

In June 1986, I got married in Birmingham and moved immediately to London to live with my husband's family. I started working doing some secretarial temp jobs in various places. Then I started to work as a secretary for a lawyer because it was £1 extra an hour and I thought I could be a legal secretary.

I learnt the legal jargon whilst temping and I applied and was successful for a full-time legal secretarial position. It was at this job that I had one of those life- changing thoughts: "I could do a better job than my boss, a conveyancing lawyer!" So I started enquiring about various courses and in September 1988 I enrolled on a four-year part-time Legal Executive course. I did my first exam whilst I was eight months pregnant with my daughter in 1990. Then I realised that with a further three years of study, I could become a lawyer and earn a good income to have a better life for my family.

Unfortunately, when my daughter was nine months old our marriage broke down. Although my husband was a brilliant father and an amazing person, sadly, we were just not the right match.

This was certainly a defining moment of my life as for the first time I had to stand on my own two feet. I was thinking, "What do I do?" I really didn't know. When I was younger, my dad dealt with the finances and then, during my marriage, my husband dealt with them. This was the time when interest rates hit an all-time high and the interest rate of the mortgage on our family home was an incredible 15%! Now being single, I was only earning £7,500 per annum as a secretary and I just couldn't make the numbers work.

My family were supportive, but were actually all devastated because I was the first person to get divorced. At the time it was completely unheard of in our community. Their solution was for me to move back to Birmingham. I knew they would be worried about what everyone else thought and I would bring an element of shame to the family, so I decided to remain in London as I also wanted my daughter to have regular contact with her father.

In September 1991, I found myself at the local housing authority benefit office asking for help. I had my daughter with me, as getting childcare was out of the question as I desperately needed financial help to get myself back on my feet. After a few hours of queuing up, I was told they couldn't help me as I wasn't entitled to any benefits because I hadn't made enough national insurance contributions. So, I was turned away.

I didn't know what to do. But I realised that I couldn't depend on anyone. My ex-husband didn't have the money at the time to help me. Obviously I couldn't ask my parents, as they wanted me to return to Birmingham. I didn't have anybody I could turn to in London. This is when I reluctantly became an accidental landlady renting out the rooms of my own house to survive, pay the bills and put food on the table.

I kept up with my studies to become a lawyer believing it would provide my daughter and I with a better life. I'd never heard of "financial freedom". That came much later as at this time my vocabulary consisted of "survival" and "a better life in the future". All I knew was that when I became a lawyer, I would earn more money.

Various people around me were saying that I didn't have the ability to be a lawyer and that I was not good enough and that I was a failure. Other people were saying that I should just give up and be satisfied with what I had. Some people questioned why I was doing what I was doing and others asked me who I was looking to prove something to. I had to learn to believe in myself and my bigger vision, remaining focused on my outcome to provide a better life for my daughter. I made that promise to her and I was determined to keep it, despite the odds against me. I had to shut out other people's negativity and I stopped sharing my dreams and goals with those people and I found a new set of friends. So, step by step, I chipped away at the various exams.

Finally in November 1996, I qualified as a lawyer. It was a very proud moment for me because all the hard work and sacrifices it took to get there had finally paid off. Just a few of the challenges while studying included: becoming a single parent during this time, losing my amazing father and, of course, still working full-time.

I built my property portfolio part-time, I'm not going to say it was easy. My journey into property was a pure accident. First of all, I started renting out the rooms of my own house. Once I qualified as a lawyer, I got a better lifestyle but I had no time.

From 1991 to 1998, my daily commute to work was over two hours and also involved dropping my daughter at school and it was very exhausting for both my daughter and I. Therefore in1998, I decided that I needed to move home. But I just couldn't let go of my first marital home as it held a massive emotional attachment for me. However, I knew I couldn't continue to live there with the journey to work each day, so I managed to re-finance my family home.

I bought my second family house. The only house I could afford was a run-down house, but it was in a good area of West London. It required timber and damp treatment, had no central heating, and the garden was a jungle. This house needed some serious TLC for sure. I remember to this day, my younger sister Gin saying I was crazy to buy such a run-down smelly house and she couldn't imagine me living there. However, I couldn't afford anything else, so I bought that house, renovated it myself with the help of friends and family who would come over at the weekends and evenings, to paint, sand doors and other DIY works.

Then, another unforeseen incident happened that knocked me back down again. I was at my boss's fortieth birthday party and over the course of the evening my non-alcoholic drink was being spiked with vodka. On my way home, I was stopped by the police and lost my driving licence for a year.

I didn't share what had happened with my family as I was totally embarrassed and humiliated about losing my driving licence. My bosses (both lawyers), and my former boss (a financial adviser) did everything to help me through the court, but it was mandatory for my licence to be taken away.

My life was devastated. I had no transport or family locally to help me, I couldn't even ride a bike. I relied on driving to get my daughter, who was now 10, to school and myself to work. I asked for help from another parent whose children went to that school who subsequently charged me petrol money to ferry my daughter to school despite no inconvenience to them.

Finally I had enough, and bought a flat closer to my daughter's school, which was also on a direct bus journey to work. I didn't end up moving into the flat as the purchase transaction took longer than expected and the thought of having to pack and unpack and put things in storage wasn't appealing. Therefore, I ended up renting it out. I saw another flat in the same block and I purchased that as well. In a way, this terrible incident is actually what started my property investment portfolio.

I was now an amateur landlady, as I now had three properties that were rented and I was earning an income from my portfolio, which I didn't even realise. The income was just going into a bank account that I wasn't touching.

I was now a full time family lawyer, earning a very good salary and I was very busy climbing up the corporate ladder and I was passionate about my clients. I used to work on child abduction, care proceedings, domestic violence and family finance cases. I won most of my cases as I went out of my way to help my clients. Life was amazing and at times I had to pinch myself to say, "Is this really my reality?"

One day, I saw an advert about becoming an armchair investor and I believed it was talking to me. I went to the seminar and I was sold into a membership package to an exclusive Property Investor Club where I would get special discounted off-plan property deals. Now I am wiser, I can see they had great marketing and sales brochures and they talked a good talk but had little else. However, at the time they appeared professional and experts in their field of property investing, with the way they handled my refinancing all my properties – including my home where I lived – to invest in these off-plan deals.

On this off-plan package, I had bought a few properties all over the UK and in Spain. Originally, the other investors and myself were promised a monthly rental of £750 per month, but then this went down to £450 after taking into account service charges and letting agent's fees. Instead of making me money, my portfolio was losing me money. I was feeding the portfolio, rather than the portfolio feeding my family and my lifestyle. This was all down to supply and demand in the area. This developer built 50 plus properties in a block and they all completed on the same day. They all looked very similar with their furnishing and layout.

Now, the tenants were in control of which property to rent because they had a lot of choice in the market place.

Myself and the other investors got nothing from these deals other than heartache, while the investment company, their lawyers, brokers and letting agents got all the returns at our expense.

Now, I had two choices. The easy option was to make myself bankrupt and walk away from the portfolio because it wasn't making money. The tough one was to somehow make them work. Actually in reality I only had one choice: I had to make them work. If I didn't and I became bankrupt I would no longer be able to practise as a lawyer, something I would not give up after it had taken me seven and a half years of hard work and sacrifices along the way and also I loved what I did.

I went out and got financially educated in property investment and then I found myself a property mentor to cement my theory into practice. Together with determination and commitment to my challenges and thinking outside the box, I turned some of the properties into lease options to deal with the issue of massive negative equity and to avoid selling them at the time for at a huge loss. I advertised for tenant buyers and vetted the candidates and chose the right people for my properties.

On a lease option I secured contracts for a fixed term of six years, for a fixed price and of course I received a monthly rental amount. I also obtained a £10,000 upfront lump sum payment to secure this deal.

I find that lease options are a great way to help someone who ordinarily would find it difficult to get onto the property ladder as it allows them time to possibly repair their credit history, save a deposit and therefore creating a win-win situation for the owner and tenant.

For the remaining properties I had to be creative to work out how to differentiate myself and my properties from all the other properties available for tenants. I got rid of the letting agents who were not doing anything to rent my properties out and I took on the job of finding tenants myself. I really didn't have the time to do this, but as I'd always dealt with my previous tenants in London myself in the past, I knew I had the skills. I was then on a mission to get these properties rented immediately.

I advertised for tenants myself. I would build up rapport with the potential applicants over the phone, ask them the relevant questions and I carried out the various tenant vetting checks to ensure I had the right tenants in my properties.

I offered longer-term tenancies at a lower monthly rent which made my properties more attractive and, because I wasn't paying letting agents' fees, I could afford the rental drop. I also provided a better quality of furnishings, with no administration fees to the tenant. This strategy paid off for me.

I have undertaken various size deals ranging from £50,000 to multi-million pounds projects all over the UK, and of course focused on various strategies such as: buy to let, lease option, house of multiple occupancy, distress, and funded such deals using various financial strategies.

We all have our challenges in life, the highs and low. In 2009, my life shifted again. When the first of two major incidents happened that changed my life forever.

The first was that I lost my high salary overnight having been made redundant during the recession. I had worked at this firm since 1993 and was now a director managing a team of lawyers. As I loved my role in family law, and property investing was still part-time, I therefore set up my own law firm. It was going really well and we won an award for working in partnership with the local Domestic Violence Unit and also I was shortlisted for the Asian Professional of the Year at the Asian Women Achievement Awards in 2009.

Then, came the second major incident. I was subject to a violent robbery, when four men invaded my home and stole everything of value, including sentimental items. The very real trauma of having my life threatened affected me so greatly that I could no longer serve my legal clients in the same way. So sadly I took the decision to close my law firm.

It was these two incidents, and my earlier incident in 1991 when I was turned away at the benefits department, that made me truly realise and believe that only you can be responsible for your own finances and well being, and we all must have a Plan B. As the bills keep coming in, how are they going to be paid?

When I went through such challenges, I sat back and re-evaluated my life and what was important and what my next steps would be.

I tell my students all the time: you don't have to be passionate about property; you have to be passionate about your life. Property is just a vehicle to get you there. The rental from my property portfolio has allowed me to deal with all these unforeseen circumstances in my life and given me time to recover, reflect and re-build my life to take me on the next stage of my life journey.

As I thought about my next step, I decided to swap my roles around. I would still keep my practising certificate so I could do pro-bono legal work and I turned my property investment hobby as my full-time passion.

Then, can you believe the awards started to flood in, such as:-

2010 - National Landlords Association Property Women Award London region NLA

2012 - Landlady of the year – London Landlord Accreditation Scheme – overall best landlord of the year award.

2013 - Shortlisted for Customer Service – Landlord and Letting Awards

2014 - Shortlisted for London Landlord Accreditation

2016 – Winner of the Landlord & Lettings Award for Landlady of the Year for the category of Social Housing.

These were a result of me not giving up, persevering and being determined to be the best landlady and to provide the best accommodation for my tenants. My tenants vary, depending on the area, and include: social housing, professionals, semi-professionals, students and corporate lets.

I consider all my tenants as my customers and treat them with respect, working with them through their difficult times. I don't just serve them with legal notices the minute there's a problem. My approach is to get them to tell me or my team what's happening, so we can see what we can do to help them and so we work together to overcome their difficult times.

The award I received in 2016 was as a direct result of the quality of my houses and the way I work with my tenants. I've got some tenants who have been with me for years. Some have lost their jobs; others have had mental health and family issues. With all of them, I've offered support for them and their families until they are back on their feet. Most of my properties are now managed by letting agents, but I managed them and work with them so my ethos about tenant support continues.

After the robbery in 2011, I have been blessed to be given a second opportunity in life and I grabbed it fully with immense gratitude. Due to the income I receive from my multi-million pound portfolio, I don't really need to work, but I would be so bored and I have a huge mission to fulfil.

My mission is to "Empower, Educate and Inspire Others" – mainly women – to take control of their financial destiny to enable them to impact the next generation.

I live my mission every single day as a property mentor, providing guidance and support to other people, mainly women, particularly property investment beginners; the novices who realise the opportunities that property investment can provide them but they don't know where to begin.

I have mentored and coached hundreds of people to get out of their comfort zone and step into the world of property investment with speed, certainty and safety. I truly believe it doesn't matter if you don't have money or have little money, whether you have poor credit, or have just come into the country. Young or old, there is a property strategy for everyone. Isn't that great news?

I run a monthly networking group called the Female Property Alliance *http://femalepropertyalliance.co.uk/* where like-minded women can meet others on the same journey and get knowledge from the expert speakers I invite. Once a quarter, we also open our doors to the men too. This is where people who are thinking of investing in property, those who have just started their journey in property investing, or are seasoned investors, all network together and share their challenges and celebrate their successes to inspire others to do the same.

I am writing a book, *Power Property Investing,* for women wishing to invest – which will be published in 2018 – explaining exactly how to get involved in property investment.

I provide training courses, both live and online, to educate others in property. I also offer property investment mentorship for individuals either one-to-one or in a group format. I know that anybody can invest in property but what I have found is that the key to success is to know realistically where you are right now and where you need to be and what steps to take to get you there safely. Everyone is an individual, so anyone seeking mentorship with my team and I, is firstly interviewed before they join our programmes to ensure they are ready and that we are able to work together to achieve their ideal outcome – because it's teamwork that makes the dream work.

As I look back at what I've achieved I am most proud of being a mother, becoming a lawyer and that I had a Plan B through property investing that saved me on too many occasions to ignore. I therefore had to share my knowledge with others and pass on my experience so that they don't have to go through the painful mistakes I have been through.

My dad used to buy property, so I guess you can say that it was in my blood. He instilled many good qualities in my siblings and I, to have a Plan B and to have integrity. My dad gave me this opportunity and I am delighted to say that finally my other family members actually get it and are now listening, and they too are setting up their Plan B for those unforeseen circumstances that life throws at us at such inconvenient and unexpected moments.

For many, the biggest thing holding people back from getting started in property investment is fear. People are terrified because of the sums of money involved and of making mistakes as everyone has some horror story they love to share. The risk and consequences of failure are too much for some people and therefore they don't do anything.

When my team and I work with a property investment mentee, the first thing we look at and teach is mindset. Some get really frustrated with this, as they just want us to teach them how to be rich while actually they don't have the right mindset to be wealthy. Therefore having all the strategies, techniques and tactics will not help if your mindset isn't programmed for wealth – or it allows you to give up at the first challenge. It's important to develop your wealth mindset for success for the long term.

With my mentees I go back to basics to clearly define what they want from property investment: when they want it by and what finances do they have available? For some, it's just extra income, others a pension, others to pay for their children's education.

Whatever your reason for financial independence, it needs to be clearly defined as: "Your Why". Your Big Why should be such a driving force that it will not allow you to quit when you hit a challenge.

I had a driving thought and I wasn't going to quit until I got it. Knowing my mentees' driving force helps me to give them direction, keep them focused and fuel their determination to keep going and not give up. Time is a big factor in property investment and will determine a lot of the decisions made, so knowing when a mentee wants to achieve their "why" is vital.

Property investment is not a get-rich-quick scheme. The days are gone when you could just buy property and make money; the tax rules have changed, the property prices are higher and the down payments are larger.

For anyone thinking of investing in property, I tell them all to get a mentor. This is not because I am one myself; it is purely because a mentor will support you and stop you making costly mistakes. My biggest regret is not having got myself a mentor sooner, as they would have saved me countless thousands and also I would have achieved my financial goals in the shortest time possible. Learning from someone else's mistakes is vital; why make them if you can avoid them? I still have a mentor today for the next stage in my property investment journey.

As I mentioned earlier, I get a massive kick out of working with beginners, rather than seasoned investors, because with seasoned investors they just need the next strategy for them, accountability and also to network with the right people. With beginners, I love seeing the journey my mentees make from being fearful to fearlessly independent, watching their success, and seeing the difference it makes to their lives. That truly gives me purpose.

I can give you countless examples of success stories that will inspire you, such as 63-year-old Malcolm, an engineer who had no pension and was scared about investing in property due to his age, lack of experience and naturally worried about making mistakes and losing his small saving pot. However, we worked together step by step and he purchased three investment properties during his mentorship. Then, out of the blue, he posted a message on my Facebook wall stating, "Thank you for an inspirational mentorship: within 12 months I have purchased 12 properties and I have a portfolio worth £1 million and I am now helping others to do the same."

Here is another story of an 18-year-old girl called Maria, who wanted to help her parents who came into the UK only four years previously, to get onto the property ladder in the West Midlands – and within four months, she was able to achieve her goal.

Another lady, Boyana, aged 29, was introduced to me by a mutual friend. She stated that she was tired of working on someone else's plan and wanted to have freedom and choices over her finances and life. She wanted to buy two investment properties on her mentorship which she achieved within five months, receiving £800 cash flow from each property. Now, they all have the tools and processes to repeat the process.

Of course, it all starts with your mindset and what money blocks you have, and how to overcome them. You could do one of the exercises I get my mentees to do. You can download this for free to get you started.

1. Exercise 1: "How to unlock your money blockages".

This short exercise is available for you here: http://www.smartcorewealth.com/sjh which will take you five minutes to complete and it will assist you to have clarity on what blockages could be holding you back from having a wealth mindset.

2. Your MP3 download "How to deal with your inner critic" is to be used as a follow up to the exercise, to handle that inner voice that could be holding you back.

Thank you for taking this short journey with me. If you would like to know more, please go to:

http://www.smartcorewealth.com/sjh

to register for free your details, and I will send you a gift in recognition of our time together.

My motto is *"If I can do it so can you."*

Dream big and I wish you all the best on your journey to success, whatever that is for you, but just remember you can achieve whatever your heart desires. I look forward to connecting with you in the near future.

PETER AND DICK DABNER

Our business is a family business at heart, and
we have family values at the core.

Peter Dabner

- 16 years' experience in the property industry.
  Sourced more than 130 opportunities for developing.
- Natural ability to think creatively and adapt to different
  market conditions.

Dick Dabner

- 41 years' experience in the property industry.
- Successfully bought, built and sold companies in a wide
  range of fields including property.
- National speaker.

Business:

Founded in 2002 by father and son team, Peter and Dick Dabner, Joint Ventures in Property is a family business that prides itself on being one of the fastest-growing property developers in Kent. They have been helping people grow their wealth since 2002.

They have a long track record in producing beautifully finished and appointed properties that, not only provide their new owners with stunning homes, but also produce significant and secure returns for investors.

Peter and Dick have been the driving force behind the growing success, in ensuring that the business employs a multi-faceted approach to property development including:

- Conversions, refurbishments and new build developments
- High-yielding rental properties
- Planning uplift
- Flipping at auction.

Services offered:

Joint Ventures
Fixed rate loans
Investing with pensions – SIPP and SSAS
Investing in SEIS and EIS schemes
Property sales, lettings and portfolio management

Email: info@jvip.co.uk

Tel: 01892 288 123

Website: www.jvip.co.uk

*

Dick: Peter and I have worked together ever since he left school. We built up a glass business, supplying decorative glass to the trade and also direct to the household, and this enabled us to buy another factory in Newmarket. In 2002, we were midway through transferring the production there to meet the demand when there was a change of senior management at the bank branch we were dealing with and they pulled our loan even though it was a government-sponsored product. They were 70% covered by the DTI and 30% by an insurance policy, so there was zero risk to the bank but they still refused to continue with the transaction.

By that time, we had started to transfer the production up to the new factory and we were left in a very difficult situation. We then had an unhappy company that we were no longer buying the factory from. They started supplying to our customers directly, and our customers were starting to slow down the payments that were due to us because they no longer needed us in the same way. We tried to claw back from where we were. We'd given notice on the leases for the properties that we had, and we found ourselves sliding backwards. I was having to sell property that I had bought over the years in order to put the proceeds into the company to prop up the business.

We didn't get enough traction to pull ourselves out of it, so we eventually had no choice but to close down the company. The accountant pointed out that we would have been better off sticking with the property that we had rather than the glass business and we should have pulled out earlier. However, we are people that never give up—we felt that we could turn the corner—and so, we didn't give up. We were over £150,000 in debt, with overdrafts and leasing deals, so we then had to find another way to make money. Peter had worked with me ever since leaving school and was unlikely to get a different job that paid enough to service the debts, and we were not prepared to go bankrupt. So, we had to figure out a way to dig ourselves out of debt. Even though Peter had a lot of business experience by that time, we now had no salaries. We had to earn chunks of money that we could pay back. During this time, Sarah Beeny and the programme Property Ladder was on television every other night, and we also had the advice of the accountant ringing in our ears.

Peter: I had that moment where I could see that property was a way forward: I'd been interested for a long while, since my father always had properties in the background throughout his years in business. I had started off when I bought my flat and then a house: instead of selling the flat, I re-mortgaged it. I dabbled in properties really as more of a hobby, but that was what the accountant pointed out. The accountant said, *"You and your dad should've probably focused more on the property, because you've made as much money as you have in the glass business but in the evenings and on the weekends. You've been working 60 hours a week in the glass business to do that."* Now I had to make a choice, as per his recommendation: the choice was to go into property full-time and see what we could do.

Dick: That was a tough time for us. It was emotionally tough as well. We were used to dealing with business situations, but when you've started from nothing and you see the staff that you've taken on and you're having to let them go—we made sure that people got paid—seeing that disintegrate was heart-breaking. Then add to that, the dawning of the fact that we had no income. We were down to a few thousand pounds left on credit cards. We knew we'd find a way of surviving, but how long would it take for this to improve? Quickly, Peter found a property in Tunbridge Wells; he'd rented in the same road when he first moved to the area, so he knew the rental demand and he managed to find a beaten-up flat to add value to.

We had to do it up and then we could get a remortgage: we scrambled any source we could get together to cover the deposit and the work to be done on it, which was minor refurbishment and looking back it wasn't a brilliant job, but it worked. We'd spent £100,000 including all the buying costs and the refurbishment and the estate agent revalued it at £120,000. We realized there was £20,000 that we could finance back out again. We could get 85% of the increased value out and start to pay our way. Not long after that, another flat next door came on the market and we said "yes" to purchasing it without really knowing how we were going to fund it, because we hadn't yet got the money out of the first property. That's when we had to go out and start talking to people to see if they could lend us some money, or what interest they might have in the deal if they did have some money.

We started to think, '*Well, other people may have money and we don't want to lose this one,*' and then another flat came up fairly soon afterwards. To work out a deal it was more of a question of going out there and finding somebody with money and then seeing what they wanted. So that's how our concept of Joint Ventures in Property emerged and it's what we're still doing to this day. People can make a loan and get an interest payment, or they can do it as a joint venture, which means that there's more of a risk, but they can share in the profit of the project in proportion to the money that they put in.

Peter: When we started, we found that first flat, but at the same time, there was a leaflet for a property course that dropped through the door. I'd rented my house out and gone back to live with Dad temporarily just to keep the overheads as low as possible. I picked up the letter about the property course and then we decided to go on it. We have always invested in ourselves in terms of business education and personal development. That course was significant because we could see that other people, who were teaching strategies that we learned on the course, were making a good living out of what we intended to do. It was "social proof", and it really gave us the impetus and encouragement to go off and find the other deals.

Other parts of business then came into play: raising the money, getting the project management sorted out, finding the exit routes so you can repay everybody, making the profit margin. So, that's how it started and we were helped a great deal by doing that course in the early days. We met some very influential people and quite soon afterwards enlisted the help of a business coach and mentor. I've always been interested in learning from people with more experience, in order to grow. I'd rather accelerate my learning by doing that than try to learn on my own.

Dick: When we started, we invited people to come and see the projects we had completed and pick our brains to see whether they would want to invest with us. Some people are out there trying to make the transition between having a job and an income and moving into full-time property. That's a much tougher decision to make than ours: we already had our backs against the wall. We had two choices: go bust or start making fast decisions without regard to whether we were going to get it 100% right or not. Therefore, in terms of our decision-making process, our thinking was simply that failure was not an option.

Peter: We just dug in. Of course, there were doubts: we were borrowing large amounts of money, and it was a leap into the unknown. There are tough decisions in property. You have to assess the risks and be as comfortable as you can be with the risks; then at some point, you have to face the situation and if you think it will work, just do it. That's what Dad was saying—we didn't really have much choice. However, we did have previous business experience and we had contacts in the building industry, as well as contacts through our previous business. We knew many people who were in the building industry that we supplied as customers. Essentially, we already had some of the skills necessary for running a business and managing the finances, and managing your finances tightly is one of the biggest jobs in the property world. So overall, we had a good start and we had the time available to start immediately.

Dick: In the early days, when we got the first flat underway, it was all fairly low key compared to what we do now. It wasn't until we established the principles and system, and had two deals in quick succession, that we needed financing. Everything started to move faster from there. We didn't want to say "no" to either of the deals, and so we had to go out and find the finance. We couldn't be shy about asking people if they had any money. Even if someone has a good idea, most people don't like the idea of asking their family or their friends, or they don't even talk to strangers about it—most people are pretty "British" about it.

We didn't have any of those constraints—we just talked to people and we found two interested prospects. One was a friend of mine who had his money put away for his tax. He was an independent business consultant and he was good enough to lend us that money. He said he didn't need it back until the following August and when we asked him what he wanted, he said, *"Well, you know, as long as you make money, just give me a slice of the profit."*

The second was somebody we'd been introduced to by Peter's mum, my ex-wife. The man had gone into her shop and started to talk about his life. He had some funds and was looking at going into property so she suggested that he talk to Peter. Then, after three meetings with Peter, this man wrote out a cheque for the deposit on one of the flats and the amount needed to do it up. He said, *"You have to sell it, I don't want a paper transaction (by which he meant a refinance). You have to prove to me that you can do it because there's more money where that came from. But you have to show me that you can do it first."*

Peter: We were working intensively. We had worked many hours in the glass business so we were used to it. Then with property, there comes a certain point when you finish your project so you can go and have a look at more properties. It's a slightly different type of work; you can spend hours trawling the Internet when everybody else is asleep (and we still do that regularly). However, when you're waiting for a transaction to complete or go through, there's only so much chasing you can do. When we didn't have many transactions going on to begin with, I suspect we probably worked fewer hours than we'd been accustomed to. They were intense and challenging times and we had a lot at stake— everything was at stake. That's how it was in the early days.

I do remember the first big refinance project because shortly after that we discovered that we could buy commercial property and convert it into residential and there was a margin in that, so we did several conversions of commercial into residential property. I remember dealing with investors in some of the early stages when we had to sell the flats in order to repay them. However, with this particular property (which was an office building converted to a house that became flats later on), I remember logging onto the bank website every 15 minutes or so to check the remortgage coming in. I couldn't believe it was happening and the remortgage was going to drop money into our bank account. I must have logged onto the bank about 30 times before I saw the money arrive. Clearly, the most important thing to do that day was to keep checking the bank! That doesn't happen any more; we seem to be busier now than we've ever been.

Dick: We just kept our heads down in the early days of JVIP, our property business. By good fortune, it was a rising market, which softened the impact of some of our mistakes such as dealing with some unreliable contractors and tradesmen in the beginning. We worked hard, and it sounds a bit strange saying it now, but we just kept doing what we were doing. Peter had started to manage most of the financial elements of it as well as finding the properties, and I started to manage the tradesmen and was out on the sites. We found that we had to have more sites going on because sometimes things stalled for whatever reason—either a property sale didn't go through quickly, or paperwork was slow, and so forth.

Peter: The basic business plan was already in place at that point. My dream at that early stage was to have a million pounds of property portfolio rented out because I could see that where we were investing in Tunbridge Wells and Kent, the property market was rising by about ten percent a year. I had this vision that if the equity was going up on a million pound property portfolio, it would go up by £100,000 pounds in a year, and if that happened, we'd soon have repaid the banks for the glass business. That was the whole basis for doing that—getting enough out of refinancing properties rather than having to sell them, then we could make a living and pay people back, and we could make sure we were meeting our obligations. These were the early goals, really. It's surprising when that happens to say, *"Okay, I've done what it takes to get to a million pound portfolio, now the goal should be* *two million."* Ultimately, the goal should be trying to buy dilapidated properties. In our third year, we came up with a new goal: to create inspirational homes. We knew that if we did that well, the money would also be there.

That was almost twelve years ago now, and we've had different strategies for different markets, and as the economy has gone through different times, we've had different strategies within the business as well. The goal has still stood though: to create inspirational homes for people.

Peter: Our business has changed and evolved. In the early days of working with investors, we saw joint ventures very much as people who were lending us money. But at some point during the journey, we saw that we could do joint ventures with people who had land and property and we found a great synergy with them. We could also add value for people in financial difficulties or in an unusual situation where we could raise the funds despite the challenge of the credit crunch and other things that have happened in the economy even when the banks stopped lending. We could still raise funding from joint venture partners; in fact, in some ways it became a little bit easier. When there was less interest being paid on people's savings accounts, they had to look around for alternatives.

We were able to put deals together and manage them so that everybody got what they wanted. We did this by matching the needs of property sellers along with the needs of the investors who wanted to put their money away safely but with a higher gain than a bank account offered. That was certainly a light bulb moment. Why would somebody sell you a property for less than it's worth, or why would he or she let you buy over the course of ten years? These are the kinds of things that we learned about during our property education. Really, when you start talking to the vendors on a practical level and see the challenges that they're facing with that particular property, it can work very well. Some people don't want the full price for their property—what they do want is a quick and efficient sale, they don't want anybody to know it's going on the market for whatever reason, or they can't afford to wait six months for a sale. There are a host of different reasons at play here. It occurred to me that my thinking would've been different if I had been in their shoes, and what's important to them can work really well for us if we can suggest a solution and manage it for them.

We've always been a business that's borrowed rather than lent money, and there's the flip side for the investors; they have a different viewpoint because they are usually the lender. There's a very specific moment I remember with one of our most active investors. We were discussing borrowing against five properties, and I put the deal forward and it was to pay it back as soon as possible, within about six months. (It's got harder now, but it was possible back then to turn things around and refinance them quite quickly.) But when our investor said that wasn't very interesting to him, I asked why because I couldn't understand that he wouldn't want his money back as quickly as possible.

He said, "Well, ideally *I'd prefer to lend you twice as much and have it in there for three or four times as long because then I don't have to keep finding another deal and doing all the due diligence. I can park my money somewhere safe. I just have to do one deal with you and I don't have to think about it for the next two years. Then in two years' time, we can sit down and talk about it again."* Before that conversation, I'd always thought that investors wanted their money out for as little time as possible and that we should be turning it around as quickly as possible. In actuality, that's not the way this particular investor was thinking. The moral of the story is that it's not always the same for other people. Everyone is in a different situation. So, that was a very distinct moment when I suddenly was hit with the idea that vendors think of things differently because of their circumstances, and investors think of things differently because of theirs. We have a business that can sit well in the middle of that.

So we are able to recycle people's money and do multiple deals with them. Even with all the money or all the project management skills in the world, you really don't have a business, if you can't find the deals. Fortunately, I've always been able to find deals that work and I've always been able to see profit margin in something—maybe from the early days of manufacturing in the glass industry, I've always been able to see something where you can spend £1 and make £1.20 of value, or more, in the end product. As we were growing the business– we work on profit margins as many businesses do—and in order to get to the higher turnover, we had to start looking at doing bigger sites. It's also certainly a lot easier to manage something that's closer to where we're based, than a site that is further away.

Dick: Now that we've done both, I know the pros and cons of managing something that's further away. We began looking for bigger and bigger sites to do within reach. We've never gone in quantum leaps, but we started looking for new-build sites. The first new-build site we did was one that we got planning permission for by ourselves: we bought a house with a big area of land to the side that was tarmacked, and we got planning permission to build two new semi-detached houses. At that point in 2007 to 2008, nobody could raise the money from the banks because of the credit crunch, although it would've been a site to sell and that was our first choice. So we thought, *'Well, there must be a way to build these houses'* and we went back to our investors and we built them ourselves.

We learned how to build property. There are many hoops to jump through to build new-build property. You need to have a warranty company that will back you and you have to have experience in order to do that—it's a different approach. It's a longer turn around as well. New-build projects often take a year or more to complete and sell, and there's no money coming in until you're at the far end of that process and things start turning to where you can cash out by selling or refinancing them. It was just another skill to learn but an important one.

Peter: Today, we focus mainly on the new-build if we can, but that doesn't mean we won't do conversions if they are good projects because that's what we did in the early days.

Dick: We try to keep it balanced as well. We still do the one-bed to a two-bed where we can convert it and add value. We'll still do a studio flat to a one-bed, and we'll also look at how we can split up one property into three flats and go back to some of our portfolio and look at how we can re-configure them to meet current market conditions. Some of the new builds do soak up a lot of finance, so you need to have cash to meet the immediate needs of the business to pay your way and pay the investors. We do have a balance of bigger projects, medium projects, and some small flips to maintain our cash flow.

Peter: We have quite a decent rental portfolio now that is profitable. We use some of the rental profit to pay investors with, which takes cash flow pressure off other parts of the business. We are also buying more HMO properties where we have income from each of the rooms, which can cash-flow a higher amount if they're managed correctly.

Dick: Before our previous business—Peter was still at school at the time—I took my children in a camper van and we finished up in Nottingham in the Virgin megastore, which I thought I'd take them to because it was an exciting new store at the time. Peter came rushing up to me and said, *"Give me my holiday money, I want my holiday money!"* I think it was £20 and I said, *"What would you want that for?"* He said, *"Just give it to me please; I really need it now!"* I said, *"What do you need it for?"* He replied, *"Well, I've just met somebody who has been given a voucher and he can't find anything that he wants and he's willing to swap his £40 voucher for £20 cash and then I can buy everything I want with the £40 voucher!"* So, that's exactly what happened. I gave him the money and he came back with the voucher and proceeded to buy just about everything in the shop that he wanted. So, we now look back and see it was a discounted deal from a motivated seller. It was a win-win, and it was really a defining moment early on in his life.

When you close the deal, complete it, and sell it, there's a buzz you get. It sounds corny to say it, but I remember the time when we built three new family houses and Peter and I walked to the office one Saturday morning and came around the corner to see the removal van outside with a family moving into one of the houses that we had built. I suddenly realised, *'that's what it is all about. We are creating homes for people and creating jobs for people—that's what it's all about.'* It came together for me in that moment. I think sometimes you're so busy that you can miss those moments.

Peter: I really get a big buzz from when we have a huge challenge and the team works really well together in the office, and then we put the right investor in place and the vendor is cooperative and you make something happen against all of the odds. That's what I think is the biggest buzz. All the people in our team are very important to us, the investors in the business, the vendors we buy or rent from and of course the people that we sell to. It's a whole community a bit like an extended family. Our business is a family business at heart, and we have family values at the core and that whole set of family values for me is what makes things worthwhile. That's where I get my biggest moments of satisfaction.

Dick: The benefits of having a family-run business are I think two-fold. First, there's a basic level of trust when you know you're shoulder to shoulder. During these last few years, it didn't all go right and there were challenges. It's about knowing instinctively that, whatever your differences, you have each other's backs. Peter and I do have our differences and people that work with us know that we can be pretty self-expressed about them. We think that's a strength, but we know instinctively that we look out for each other and that we have the business at heart and we are prepared to give up our point of view in the favour of our work. It always works better if someone else can suggest an alternative viewpoint. It makes it sound easy, but when we have different skillsets, that's sometimes difficult to do. Still, I think I can count on fewer fingers than on one hand when we have gone to bed on an argument. We are committed to that not happening, and we clear things up before it's lights out and the next day starts.

Peter: I think that's a huge advantage and it'd be very difficult to have if you didn't have that family bond. That's something that's built on our core values and it's very important to me as well that we don't ever disagree over things to such an extent that we have to go to sleep at night thinking we've fallen out over that. That's the motivation.

Dick: I think another thing that tends to happen is that we seem to gravitate towards other family businesses. Some of our best contractors are family businesses, and we do have a benchmark because we will try people out and if, for instance, those contractors, suppliers, even those investors, don't share the same values, they don't last long. If they aren't willing to show fairness, or they don't handle challenges in a positive way, we don't work with them for very long and they paint themselves out of the picture.

Peter: If you go into business as family, you have to put different "badges" on. We've had a business mentor now for over seven years who has witnessed our biggest growth at JVIP and he started the concept of: when you step into a meeting, you put different badges on. We'll always be father and son, but in a meeting one of us is investor relations and the other operations, or a director and a director. You have to see things from a business standpoint at times. People sometimes find it funny that I call my father "Dick" and refer to him as "my father"; I don't call him "Dad" at work and that's something that's come about as a result of our mentor saying he doesn't want to hear that. Out of the office he is still "Dad" but at work, he is my business partner.

We keep the family mode alive at the end of the day by closing the business off, going out, having a meal together, and socialising. In these moments, he's definitely my dad. But at the office, or in this meeting room, around this table, we're responsible for the needs and goals in the business. That's something that's quite different. I think that can definitely take some getting used to.

Dick: What's unusual as well is that I'm actually a third of the business and Peter is two-thirds, so Peter will have the final say. Although I'm often seen as the front of the business, it's the other way around, and I have to accept that. For example, if Peter disagrees with my recommendation, I will back down on it. It doesn't happen that often, but there are circumstances where it does.

Peter: When you have a business and it can help other people, it's motivating because it's a pleasure to be able to give some of the proceeds of what we do to help other people. We have a privileged lifestyle and it's great to be able to have a business. It comes with its challenges, but it's a huge opportunity that some people never get. We've helped various charities over the years and we always help where we can, particularly coming up to the end of the year and at Christmas time. The whole office has the opportunity to give towards charity and we always make a contribution as a business One charity we support is called Msaada that rebuilds communities that were broken after the genocide in Rwanda, and then there's another charity that's close to our hearts which supports people with Down's Syndrome. Another time Dick met a little boy through one of our investors, and this child has spina bifida. We were able to fund a much-needed piece of equipment that he could have at home that's helped him rehabilitate on a far better basis than if he could only use it once a week when he went to the rehabilitation centre. So, all of these things are important to us.

Dick: I don't think there's one big thing that I could say I'm the most proud of. We help in little ways and in big ways when we can, and we help a variety of people and causes, ranging from the families of people who work for us to external charities.

Peter: In terms of being most proud businesswise, I take a lot of pride in taking the property we have, maximizing the sites, seeing how to get the most use out of the space and the property, and then ultimately seeing the finished product. I enjoy seeing something that we've taken from concept to completion.

Dick: When people come down to see us and they're new to the property game—maybe they don't have any property yet—we take them around and show them what we've done, how we've done it, and where we started. Then, some time later, we might get an email from them saying they were inspired and have now started in property. It certainly gives me a real buzz to know that we've inspired people, to show them that anything's possible.

There is one thing I have to say to anyone wanting to achieve success in property: make yourself accountable to somebody and never give up. In our case, it may have been easier because we've had each other and we are accountable to each other, but as we've grown the business we've taken on a business mentor, and we are accountable to him. Even though he doesn't tell us how to run the business, he holds us accountable for what we say we're going to do and what we've agreed to do. We learned that having a business mentor is important through being on property courses and doing lots of assignments. Find somebody who is going to hold you to account for what you say you're going to do, because otherwise human beings will "slip under the wire" and not do it. In this particular business, if you don't keep doing what you say you're going to do, you won't get the deals, you won't find the investors, you won't deliver the projects, and you won't have the reputation. Find somebody that you can be accountable to.

Peter: I agree, and I would reiterate the concept of never giving up. The other thing that's very dear to me, and a concept I try to live by, is that you have to look after yourself so that you can in turn look out for others. If you're not physically well, you can't contribute what you should contribute to a family business, or to anything, really. For me, I like to go out for a run or to the gym because it gives me a chance to think and plan what I'm going to do from a business point of view. We went to the gym together this morning; we try and do that at least once a week, if not twice a week, so that we look after our health.

I feel so much more mentally clear when I exercise regularly and it's something I've heard other people say as well. It gives me the chance to reflect and make plans. I'm also a big believer in not just keeping a to-do list, but an actions list that is continuously managed as well. Try to tick those actions off daily and make progress. We also set annual targets and a three-year rolling programme of targets which we review regularly and we then break that down into years, quarters, months, and weeks of what we have to achieve. You need to stay focused: are you still achieving what you want to achieve and carrying forward actions to make sure they happen? I think it's very easy for the time to slip past and suddenly weeks turn into months and into years, so you have to make sure you're always monitoring progress against a strategic plan.

Dick: I think we always like to offer encouragement to anyone wanting to get started in property–it's not rocket science and anybody can do this if they put their mind to it. I think that's what I would say. Learn from other people's mistakes and successes.

Peter: When the biggest challenges occur, those are also the biggest opportunities. Examples of these situations are the credit crunch or cash-flow challenges in a business. If it was easy, everybody would be doing it and there wouldn't be a margin in it. So you have to find the answer and keep yourself thinking outside the box and try to maintain a work-life balance so you're level-headed. You've got to have a frame of reference: your health and fitness, family, and the business. Look at challenges as opportunities and see what you can turn them into, because if you can solve a bigger challenge that's stopping other people, there will be a way to make money from that

Dick: Year after year, we've found that if we can solve somebody else's problem, we can get what we need and they get what they need. So, it's a mindset thing that you have to keep working on to make a difference. And if you're making a difference, then there's a strong chance you will succeed–whether it's in property or anything else.

Peter: That's a good point. When we're talking to investors, we want to find out what's important to them. When we're talking to those who want to sell or buy property from us, we learn what's important to them. You could boil it down to the idea that we often put ourselves in other people's shoes. Now, of course, we have a business goal, which is important and it has to be in context for the business, but actually, it's about what the other people want. If you can solve that problem, or meet a need, that's a powerful way to work.

Dick: We are always looking for new challenges, new investors and new projects; and welcome opportunities wherever they show up.

JULIA SCOVILLE AND CHRISTINA YAKOVLEVA

Having children changed everything, because a corporate career and children don't go well together

Business: City One Group: Investors, Property, Lettings.

Services offered: HMO conversion. Armchair investment.

Email: julia@cityonegroup.co.uk

Facebook: www.facebook.com/cityonegroup/

Website: www.cityonegroup.co.uk

*

Julia: We always ask our clients: "What is your property dream?" Not the dream you had last night ;) but a dream you would like to achieve in property? Would you like to have one property in your portfolio, 100 properties, or no properties? Where do you see yourself living? In England, Spain, Barbados or Grimsby?

I always wanted to invest in property, but I had an obstacle – MONEY. I believed you had to have lots of money to do it. I thought to myself, *'Well, to save up a deposit for the first BTL house is going to take me about ten years. That's really a long time, but maybe that's what I should do: each day put money aside and then at least I'll have something.'* How wrong was I?!!!

I was a very career-oriented woman with a nice salary, BMW as a company car, a laptop etc —what could be better?

It was my son's 2nd birthday. I woke up early in the morning; he still was asleep. I looked at his beautiful face, but couldn't wish him "Happy Birthday" or say "Good Morning" as I had to rush off for my early commute to London. My son went to nursery with a caterpillar birthday cake, and I remember sitting at work thinking, *'Has he eaten his cake yet? Did he enjoy it? I wonder what he's doing right now.'* I only saw him in the evening on his birthday. I remember thinking that this wasn't right. I couldn't picture myself living like this; I really wanted to instill my values in my child, not let someone else instill theirs. Having children changed everything, because a corporate career and children somehow don't go well together.

I recalled the title of the book, "*Feel the Fear and Do It Anyway.*" I started exploring different options. I saw a newspaper advertising a free, two-hour seminar in London. That course opened my mind completely and changed the way I was thinking about property investment.

Christina: Someone said: "Follow your dreams and your heart" and I truly believe this is the way to live your life fully, feel happy and add value to other people's lives. My dream was to have a big happy family, good income and travel a lot. Pretty simple, yeah? So I lived in few countries, I studied a lot, got a good job, got married and felt life was wonderful

But there is the life before and after you have kids, right? So everything changed for me after I had my daughter. It really hit me when I had to go back to work! We just don't really know what it's like do we? I promised to come back full-time and I did, but, obviously, I quickly changed my mind. I then had to wait a looooong six months until my part-time hours had been approved. So I got it! Straight away, I felt really down not to be in control of my life and I didn't really have a choice. On top of that, sadly, my relationship had broken down and I had no idea what I was going to do. How was I going to make a living by myself? Who would take care of my daughter if something happened to me? So I started looking for the answers to my question: how could I earn good income and have flexibility? I started thinking more about passive income so I could spend time with my daughter and be with her when she had her first smile, her first tooth, her first step. I didn't want to miss it! So, I went to study ... again. But this time, it was different! I was learning about properties: how to invest, all strategies from rent-to-rent to new-build and commercial development. I knew straight away that this was the only way to get income, security, flexibility and growth. And in the meantime, I met Julia before my first training course (on a gymnastic class for kids).

Julia: "The Clearer the Dream – the Closer the Goal!" Our Goal was £5,000 per month cash flow from businesses and leaving our JOB. For the first nine months, we went to nearly every single learning provider in England, we analysed all strategies, researched the market, observed, met other investors and built our power team. After lengthy preparation, we set up three companies, bought our first house with none of our own money, finished five projects for our clients and, finally, left our jobs! We just took a massive action. We didn't even finish the course, before we started securing our first client!! We were both very determined.

If you are really prepared to change your life, change your future and your children's future, it is possible, but you have to do something different. Remember the old saying, "If you keep doing the same thing, you will get the same results."

I should highlight a couple of points that stood out along our journey. The training courses always mention that you can become financially free in six months' time. We thought, *'Oh, that sounds really good. We can be financially free in six months' time, brilliant, let's do it.'* Four months down the line and we were not even near buying our first property or being financially free and we felt the pressure. By month six, we were in the same position and starting to feel quite negative and like we had failed. We were thinking, *'How come other people can do it, but we can't? What we are doing wrong?'* We weren't about to give up, but it was that point when we started thinking, *'Maybe this is not for us.'*

Then I said to Christina, *"Look, let's review what we're doing and what the problem is,"* and it became apparent that this six-month timeline was putting pressure on us. It wasn't realistic, and we decided to take the pressure off ourselves and remove that six-month timeline. We knew investing in property made sense, as well as being in the property business, so it didn't matter when— as long as we kept going and kept going, we knew that it would come out right at the end. Just, "Don't give up! Review and move on."

There came a tremendous sense of relief from that simple change of mindset. Within the next three months, we secured our first client with an HMO conversion project and we found our first angel investor! We started running HMOs tour days and attracting lots of people to come and have a look at what we were doing.

City One Group Today:

Christina: We work well together as a team. We both bring a mix of skills that complement each other and bring lots of value to our businesses. Julia is our people person! She aaaabsolutely loves people. She's our relationship manager, public speaker, and "mum" to all our residents, looking after our letting side and all our clients.

Julia: Christina has three degrees. She has degrees in physics, accountancy, and tourism. Her strength lies in numbers, so she's our analyst and " City One Computer," as we call her. She really can support opportunities in terms of finances, planning, and structure. She says, "Check the figures and follow your gut feeling."

The combination between us is great. Someone said we are "*a match made in heaven!*"

We established our model of HMOs and created brand loyalty: it is a high-end boutique-style HMO, so we only attract professionals or young people who just graduated from university who have got their first job and would like to live in a really nice environment. We wanted to create a different experience for people who will be living in our properties. We want them to feel at home, with the idea that if they feel at home, they will stay longer. If we always have communal areas and promote socialisation, they will develop a sense of a friendly community and will be less likely to move out. There are likely to be fewer arguments in the house, too. So, we focus on high-end HMOs.

We became experts in what we do and love it – we help people to achieve their dreams through properties. For some it will be passive income to go on extra holidays, for some it's a financial future for their children. We offer services to clients who would like to invest in properties, but do not have the knowledge or time to do it. We help them to make passive income using our expertise and providing a hassle-free service for them. Most of our clients work in the city and some of the clients are travelling all over the world, so there is just no way they can do it themselves, and that's how we can help. The other way we help is to collaborate with angel investors, who are not in the position to own their own investment property but still can benefit from property acquisition.

Our motto is: Pilot your life to your financial freedom!

SUSANNAH COLE

I knew I wanted security – and even with these pretty decent jobs, as a single parent the money just stretched to about the end of the month.

Susannah Cole is highly respected in property investing circles. She is a well-established property investor who has a very successful flipping strategy, and owns a substantial HMO and single let property portfolio.

She started The Good Property Company in 2011, as a kitchen table start-up. In the first five years of being full-time in property, she and her team have sourced more than 200+ properties, all in Bristol, with a value of over £45 million, at a purchase price of £30 million (before refurb).

Not bad for a start up! Susannah loves to share how to get to (almost) financial freedom. Financial freedom is freedom of both money and time. The almost bit is because nothing is ever perfect, but by sourcing discounted deals, owning property assets that pay rent monthly, doing buy to sell, and putting a huge amount of work in the early days, you can come out the other end with an income stream that needs very little time.

Straight speaking, chocked full of content, and passionate to share her knowledge, to help you either get started in your property journey, or improve where you are currently at.

Business: The Good Property Company

Services offered: Property Education

Phone: 0117 942 8914

Website: www.thegoodpropertycompany.co.uk

*

I had a very brief spell as a waitress, during which I embarrassingly spilled tomato soup on somebody's lap. But after this, my first job was starting a dance night when I went to St Andrews University. I love dancing, and St Andrews is a very quiet place with only one place to dance on Thursday nights, so I started a dance night. It was very scary because I'm very above-board and I had all of these very shady characters coming up to me and really didn't want anything to do with their world.

So, that was my first shot at being an entrepreneur. After I graduated, I had my daughter very young, when I was 22, and it would have been quite difficult to have a job at the same time to bring in income. So instead of going into a job and then struggling with childcare, what I did was start a business. It was my second business, if you will. I started a Fair Trade business, because I believed and I still do believe very strongly in fairness, so I was very enthusiastic and evangelical about Fair Trade, while being very upset by the differences between the first and third world. I ran the Fair Trade business about 20-odd years ago, so it was quite a new thing at the time. I was working with suppliers who imported crafts, clothing, musical instruments, furniture and jewellery from third world countries that were all classified as Fair Trade.

I ran the Fair Trade business for seven years from the age of 22 to 29. I started with a little painting table, one of those fold-out tables, at a little craft fair, and then grew it and grew it, ending up with five shops in Scotland. We also had a three-and-a-half-ton Dodge van going out to lots of different festivals most weekends. Our work schedule got quite full, but I grew the business just by watching cash flow and never taking on any borrowings. I worked from the shed in my house. My kids would be at playschool – I had two kids by then – and I'd have the washing on in the background, because obviously with two little kids you're constantly washing. So, they'd go to playschool and I'd work like crazy before picking them up, then again once they were asleep. I would plan a month's cash flow in advance, and then we'd sell that and plan the next month's cash flow for the shops.

Then after that, I decided I probably needed some skills, so, conscious of that need I looked for a job, because I knew that I'd learned loads bootstrapping and so forth. You don't take on debt when you bootstrap, because you build yourself up by your bootstraps as an entrepreneur. I knew that I'd learned everything through experience, so I thought I probably needed some professional skills. I got this interesting job for an economic agency supporting the cashmere industry in the Scottish Borders. It was really useful to attain a wider level of understanding and view of economics, and to then go in and advise 14 client companies at the Director and Chief Executive level. I saw the difference between the most successful textile staff firms in Europe and companies that later were going bust – it was always about the management. It was always about the skills of a handful of people: the Chief Executive, the Sales Director, the Finance Director, the Operations Director. They didn't have Marketing Directors, and that was a major flaw. The failure or success was always due to the top team. People in the company obviously play a big role, but if the top team is neither competent nor talented with skills, you can bet your bottom dollar the business won't succeed.

I sat on companies' boards: because as the economic development agency was putting a lot of money into them, they needed us. I was there to identify where we could best support them. It was tough because they didn't necessarily always appreciate a 29-year-old female's point of view — which is an understatement. We also did some international marketing campaigns in South Korea and Japan, and I raised a lot of European money to support the industry. Here, we had to analyse the industry and try to analyse each company to see where we could best help, but we had to work with people who were already in place. In other words, we had a lot of support to offer, but limited power to influence directly.

After that, I did a couple more jobs I really enjoyed and got more skills from a start-up youth volunteering charity in Scotland that grew really fast. I was also the sales director for a radio station, so I was running KISS in Bristol. But I knew I never wanted to have more than four jobs. In hindsight, everything tracks back as if it's a straight line, but of course it never is. It's always chaotic as you're going forward, but I knew I only wanted four jobs at most because I knew I was probably unemployable long-term because I don't like being told what to do!

Also, I knew I wanted security — and even with these pretty decent jobs, as a single parent the money just stretched to about the end of the month. I was very conscious about pensions and aware I was going to work crazy hours, have a relatively small pension, and not see my kids as much as I wanted to. I knew there had to be a different way, because I was Head of Household and raising two children, and because I needed to have a strong salary for the family since there weren't two of us earning. I therefore had many responsibilities, which meant I wasn't seeing the children as much as I wanted to, and I'm very family-focused. I knew it had to change. I started reading up about property, having always loved it. I had looked at property for years but never felt able to commit until I did four home renovations.

For two and a half years, the kids and I would live in dust, then the house would become beautiful and I'd sell it and we'd move to another. Each time I doubled our money. It sounds like I planned it, but I didn't. I just loved it. Then we moved down to Bristol, when the children were older for them to enjoy the city. Up until then we had lived these beautiful, idealistic, Enid Blyton-like days. The last house we lived in was two miles out of a village, and I'd open the gate and say, "Off you go." Then I'd see them at teatime. I'd be gardening with 20 vegetable patches over two and a half acres in the garden, and the kids would just be rolling across the hillsides and then would be back for tea. It was beautiful for young children, but not great for teenagers, and I knew we needed to move to a city so they could be engaged.

When we moved to Bristol, I was able to buy a property there and then take £60,000 out for my mortgage, and buy my first buy-to-let. The main thing that drove me was wanting to spend time with my children and worrying about my pension. That motivated me to go to seminars to find out about property and read up on it. I'm an independent person, so I read. I read about property for a full year really intensively. The first book I read was Andy Shaw's book, *Money for Nothing ... and Your Property for*

Free. It wasn't the best-written book I've ever read, but it was the first book that kind of showed me that it could be done. It was very exciting to read about and appreciate that success in property was a possibility.

The first property I bought was a one-bed flat five minutes from my house. It was £79,000, and at the time I knew it was worth about £100,000 – £120,000 and was a £7,000 or £8,000 refurbishment. I was absolutely beyond terrified all the way to buying it, but within 30 seconds – it only took 30 seconds to walk around the property – I thought, "Right, fine, where's the next one?" Once you've done it, you think, "Well, I can do it."

It's always more scary before you do something than when you do it because once you do it, you think, "We're going to renovate this out, and then move on to the next." I'm still friendly with my very first tenant, too. He's a lovely guy. It was absolutely the right investment. "Now I know how to do this," I thought. I've always bought discounted. Always. What I'd been reading was that you could do it again and again and again. Buy discounted, refinance, pull all or some of your money back out again. That was what was really critical to me because I only had £60,000, so I had to live by the whole theory that I'd read in books that said you can get some or all of your money back out again.

In the first year, I bought three houses because I was still working a full-time job, and obviously wanted to remain committed to delivering well. The second year, I bought four houses in the first six months because I was still working full time. So, during the first 18 months – I bought seven houses in 18 months – I had to borrow some money. I jumped out of my job, and the second I jumped out of my job we then sourced 43 properties that year. It was hair-raising and super scary, but it's not hard to see the difference that going full time made. I had actually set a target of 60, so I was quite disappointed. We more or less did between 40 and 60 properties every year as a sourcing business, and every year I was also the biggest buyer in the sourcing business.

Along that journey, there were times when I asked myself what on earth I was doing on a daily basis. The biggest hurdle was money, which I think most people probably feel the same way about. What I did then was I actually very quickly went and raised money, because I had read all the books, and by that point I'd started to go to property investor meetings in Bristol. I listened to all the speakers and took a lot of mental notes, thinking I'd just do what they told me to. Of course, they were talking about refinancing: no money left in. Initially, I had no intention of using anyone else's money. I was naïvely going to use my £60.000, recycle it again, and again, and again, and then the 6-month rule was brought in. It was just after the recession had begun when I started buying.

The 6-month rule meant that I could only probably do two properties every six months, and that was nowhere near fast enough for me. When I started in property investing, I had thought, "I'm nailing it. Let's do this." So that was kind of disappointing. At that point I decided that the hold-up was money and that I would have to fundraise. I raised £600,000 in 14 weeks. It was quite scary, because at that point I was paying fairly high interest rates. I paid £72,000 in interest in my first year, but at this point I had dropped my salary to between £700 and £900 a month. It's a fairly strong risk, but I think the work I'd done on the Fair Trade business years ago, when we worked from month to month and cash flow was critical, really helped me.

I was on top of cash flow every single day, just to make sure things were what they were. I was projecting out 18 months in advance. Money was the first priority, but the main game changer was having the time, though I didn't appreciate that until I looked back with hindsight. Now, I mentor people, and you really see that time's a game changer. It was when I made a full-time commitment to it that things really took off for me by a factor of 10.

There were challenges of course along the way. I've made many dummy moves, but I made a really dummy move with my second purchase. I bought a house with an aluminium roof at auction with a mortgage, which is probably not something I would suggest that anybody does if they want to sleep for 28 days. That was not clever, but I was very fortunate it went through okay. Otherwise, I would have had to switch to bridging finance because I was so naïve at the time. I didn't appreciate the details of funding. Oddly, I always find that any challenge ends up being the best thing that could have ever have happened to me; it just takes about a year and a half to appreciate that perspective. If the 6-month rule hadn't come in, I'd have used my £60,000 again and again, and wouldn't have been forced to learn the skill of fundraising. I wouldn't have been so hungry to fundraise because I wanted to build a portfolio faster, and I wouldn't have achieved the end result.

There was a lot of trial and error. I met three experienced property people that were incredibly helpful, and this is what I love about our industry. Because you and I are unlikely to buy the same house; therefore we're better off helping each other. We're not in direct competition, we're not trying to take 33% of the industry. Nobody owns 33% of British houses; the number of houses even I own is like a drop in the ocean.

People who have done well like to see other people grow too. I had three guys in the early stages that were courteous enough to talk to me as if I knew something when I knew absolutely nothing, and that's one of the main reasons we've published so much material for free. It wasn't just that they gave me lots of information: it was that they treated me like an equal. You go into this industry feeling that there's all this status and standing, but there actually isn't. This business is self-employment and building assets. No one ever needs to know how many assets you have – it's of no importance to anyone but you and your accountant. For business leaders I looked up to, to treat me as equal despite the fact that they had hundreds of houses was so honourable that I wanted to perpetuate that.

Later on, when I was just about to jump from my day job, it was crazy. I was shattered doing full-time work and the property – because I did 40 to 60 hours for my day job, and then another 30 hours in property. There's no other way to do it: you've got to put the time in. I was pooped. I went down to Vanish Patel's meetings on Monday nights, and my children were old enough that I would leave food on the Monday night. I'm very family-focused, so Sunday was dinner and family day. Saturday, they're like, "Mum, you're just not cool enough" and would hang out with their friends. On Monday night I would go down to the meeting and Vanish asked me to do a presentation. I told everyone, "I'm going to do 60 deals," and I think he just thought, "Oh, I'm going to have to look after her." He's been my mentor ever since. There are times when we have really encouraging conversations, and there are times when I just get on the phone and can't breathe because it's so worrying or stressful. It was so in the past, though not so much now. I've never felt like giving up, but there have definitely been times when I felt like lying down for a moment. There was a time where I actually did lie down on the floor for comic relief and comedy head-banged the floor.

By this time, we had small teams, so I worked a lot with Ash, who did a lot of our sourcing for almost six years. He's a lot more relaxed than I am, and I'm a lot more driven than he is. We'd find that if I was up, he was down. If I was down, he was up. It was a really nice, symbiotic relationship, so in that particular instance, I literally lay on the floor and head-butted the floorboards because life was so unfunny. He just said, "Yeah, we'll get through this." It was so useful that somebody was just outright saying it, but now I understand that you really just don't give up. There's always a solution. It's simply that you can't figure it out straight away. Isn't it grit that lets you get knocked down seven times, and get up eight?

Today, my business is a blessing, and the stress is reduced. I don't think I ever once bought a house when I had all the money or knew I had all the money, because it's like running. You're always moving forward. Now, it's much, much more securely based. It was never insecure, because there was a very clear plan with strong checks and balances, but I was growing at a rate of knots and it was quite full-on.

At one point, we were renovating 30 houses at a time. You can just imagine my brain. So now, for the first time ever, I'm taking a very brief pause in buying. I'm at the 10-year mark: you sprint for nine years, and then take a breather. It's like a lot of sports: you train for a number of days and then you have a rest day. This year, it's really fun and bizarre to even think about the portfolio we have: single-lets, multi-lets, some serviced accommodation. We're still building houses, we're still doing buys and sells, and I've got a chapel I'm renovating next. I've just finished a great house with no roof. Instead of doing between 5, 10, 30 buys and sells at once, for the first time ever I just have one to focus on, which is amazing and a pleasure.

What we're now doing is looking at this set of assets and continually working on and improving them. It's exciting. Now, that won't last because I will definitely go on my next growth spurt, but it's really fun to take this period of time to make everything as efficient and effective as possible, and to start very strongly reducing down loan-to-value to look at some of the key investor indicators. I looked at loan-to-value, yield and net profit at the beginning, whereas now I look at things like age plus loan-to-value being less than one hundred. I look at when we are going to make the houses unencumbered, and when that domino effect will move from house to house. My next ambition is to just buy with cash from here on out. It's a blessing to be steady on the first mountain top and not be running uphill, out of breath, panting.

There are two main places where I am directing my energies in my business right now. I'm still building a house at the moment, and then I've got another major refurbishment to start, so there's a portion of my week where I'm overseeing renovations, which I really enjoy. I like making things happen and making them happen very effectively and cost efficiently. There's no room to mess around. I chase my tradesmen like the wee Scotswoman I am. "When are you going to be there?" "Great. You're definitely going to be there?" "Okay. Wonderful. Can't wait to see you there." "Great, you're there tomorrow aren't you? Wonderful. Thank you so much."

I do this even though they're good lads – and they really are – because renovations are a much bigger part of my diary than ever before. I don't do anything to do with my own properties in terms of the day-to-day management, but I work very closely with the team to make sure we hit all of our KPIs (key performance indicators). We've got very clear KPIs for each of our businesses. For example, we have 10% of rent roll going to repairs, and only five repairs outstanding at the end of each month. We want a very high occupancy rate; we're less than 2% void rate at the moment on the portfolio, and I want to improve that. We're looking at how we can keep that as profitable as humanly possible, and then we try to challenge ourselves to make it even better, which is really good fun.

There's more focus on the assets than previously. Not in a day-to-day, me doing the work way, but involving me working with the team. The second part, which I also love as you've probably gathered, is the mentoring and teaching. We've got quite a strong number of online education courses and packs. We've got packs, we've got audio, the workshops we put in film and audio. I like to produce high-quality work – whatever it is – and I want my work to be something someone could really get as much knowledge as possible from, just by buying it.

I really enjoy producing these, and I still have two mentoring groups. I have a face-to-face group, which is just a fabulous one. It's quite high-level and high-performing, with 80% of experienced people already owning property, and it's growing pretty fast. Then I also have an online mentoring group – we give them the online curriculum and I still take conference calls for those guys. In terms of the training, I do weekly conference calls with each of my two groups and the very occasional workshop. I run the two mentoring groups, and then I produce good-quality material online if they're little library geeks like me who sit and read in an armchair. It's kind of half and half – I get fired up by both property development and management education.

If anybody else wants to achieve what I have, my first piece of advice is to realise that success is not a great distance away from you. There is that saying that you are the average income of the five closest friends you hang around with, and how many of us know millionaires on a social basis? There's nothing much different about millionaires from anyone else, except that they got up and went for it, and obviously had the business acumen to make it happen.

In retrospect, the first 'aha' moment is realising success is not such a distant goal. Do not ever think it's out of your reach. I was a single parent just making ends meet, and now I'm in a very fortunate and grateful position. It is absolutely within your reach, but just takes a massive amount of growth and a few years to get there.

The second necessity is grit. Angela Ducksworth wrote a really good book, *Grit*, because she wanted to figure out why people were successful, and she reckons it's a combination of passion and perseverance. So, I have a complete passion for property ten years on. I will still stop and lose my breath when I see a beautiful property or beautiful interior. I like the grit involved in making sure the builders are doing what they're supposed to when things go wrong. It is the getting up after a knock that builds character; you have to know that failures are normal.

I make sure in my teaching to never pretend we've been super successful without loads of mistakes, because I want my pupils to see all the things we failed on so it normalises things going wrong and they realise it's part of the journey. Success is not out of your reach: it just involves determination to keep going. Get up after a knock, and when you have rejection or difficulty, figure out another way.

The third thing, which is probably more property-specific, is to always do your figures and to always have a plan A and B. If you're going to sell, make sure you don't buy something that's going to give a crappy yield. If you're going to sell, I want you to have a 20% mark-up minimum, after all costs. Don't fool yourself either. Do 45 pieces of comparative research before you buy the property, but at the same time, I don't want you having a buy to sell that will only yield 4%, as a rental fall back position. That's terrible. I want you having a buy to sell that, if you had to keep it, would give you a 10% yield and give you all or most of your money back. You are faced with a lovely first-world problem: "Gosh, do I make money when I sell, or do I make money by keeping it and refinancing it?" Always have a plan A and plan B, because property is very cash-intensive. You're like a great big ship that slowly turns around, not a little speedboat that can nip around in a minute. So you need to protect your back by having a plan A and a plan B.

My fourth piece of advice is to take on board, but ignore the "noise" in the external world in which you're operating – P.E.S.T.L.E., the Political, Economic, Social, Legal, Technological, and Environmental atmosphere. Be aware of it and analyse it. Of course, you can't really influence any of these things. You're like a little boat bobbing along the waters of that external economic world that you're in.

The reason you do this analysis is because you have to ask, "What does this mean for me? What can I do about it?" At all times, in any property cycle or any government atmosphere, there are rumours and things being legislated against landlords or investors that make it difficult. Rules also change. Then a bunch of people throw their hands up and say it's too hard. Ignore the fact that someone is saying it's too hard, and try and figure out how you go past that difficulty in your business and keep moving forward. Inevitably, the external environment is something you as an entrepreneur need to navigate and not get blocked by. I don't quite mean to ignore it, because then you wouldn't be tooled up to be able to deal with it, but just damn well move past it effectively.

When I started, I bought in a recession. All my friends, including my very savvy business friends, thought I was completely nuts. Of course, now I look very clever, having bought in a recession. At the time, property was going down the drain and everybody thought it was a dreadful investment. So plough your own furrow after analysing the environment you're in, and figure out your response to it while ignoring the noise.

If I had to give advice about the first step to take before investing in property, I would genuinely say to get educated, whether you're little geeks like me and read loads of books or are more social. The big game changer for me was moving from going to a property meet once a month to attending once a week, because I got to meet loads of people and therefore learned loads more things. You definitely have to be reading books and magazines and attending events. You have to be writing your business plans down even if you don't believe they could happen.

I did these things and still do them on a regular basis. Suddenly you go, "Oh wow, I'm much closer to that than I realised." By writing it, it becomes concrete, because then you figure out all the reasons why you can't do it. They're just gaps in time, money and skills. There's no reason you can't do anything. You say, "I'm going to buy all these houses." Okay, you've got a gap of money. Now, write a fundraising campaign. "I've got a gap of time." Great. Employ a couple of people and write a fundraising campaign. "I've got a gap of skills." Great. Educate yourself, get a mentor. Writing things out is like massaging muscles, it's just a knot, and you massage the knot out by figuring out and writing out how you bring that resource into your business.

Over the years, there have been moments that I've been particularly proud of. I look back and I wipe my brow, and I'm so damn grateful. But what's weird about property is that you just get on with your day-to-day life, and you forget how much property you own. My ego's not necessarily built around my net worth. My stability is, but not my ego. I was with my cousin, who now owns ten properties, and I was proud of her beyond belief. I just thought it was genuinely and absolutely amazing. I spent the day with her, then drove away from her family home and realised that I've got significantly more. I was so damn impressed with her and her husband's achievements because you forget how many you own, because you just get on with it. Overall, it's less about pride and more about the lovely feeling of safety in my stomach.

It's just so nice to feel that unless you do something really stupid, you're actually okay. I think the main thing I'm grateful for is my ability to choose. I like a little sport, and I fancy a good laugh. I do Olympic weightlifting, which I know wouldn't be easy to guess because I'm five feet two and slim, but I somehow just got into it. You choose the number of hours you take. I went for brunch last week with a friend. When Sonny, my coach, got picked to go to the Olympics, I immediately went to Rio to support him. My son has moved to Barcelona now and said, "Mum, when are you coming?" I'm like: "Great! I'm going to go over for two weeks now." It's the ability to have a choice that's amazing. That's more my being grateful than proud, but I am glad that I was able to deliver that to myself.

Sometimes I look back to how it was at the beginning when I was a single parent worrying about money and my pension. I remember watching an episode of *Sex in the City* and it being so funny, but falling off the sofa because I started laughing and was so tired. I couldn't keep going. Raising children is gorgeous, but it's tiring. Having 100% responsibility for their wellbeing is both wonderful and really scary. I just keep looking back and thinking how very pleased and grateful I am.

I recommend property, because it is absolutely life-changing. I hope that I can be a role model to my children, and pass on my lessons to them. My daughter worked in the business for a year, and I hope that her doing so subtly allowed her to pick up pieces of knowledge without her mum telling her directly. She also did my mentor programme for a year, and I hope that really helped her. My son has worked in the business every summer during his college years, so I strongly hope it helped him. I just have to be very conscious that I don't try to pass on "my rules for me, my rules for you" to my children, even though I'd love to. Wouldn't it be amazing if you just told them what to do because their lives would be safe then? But you have to let them grow by themselves. I intend fully, when my kids are 30, to be gifting them property, but not until that age – I don't want them getting it too early. Got to have a little grit to make that pearl!

KEVIN WRIGHT

The Secrets of How to Recycle Your Cash

Broker. Educator. Speaker. Judge for Property Investors Awards: 2016, 2017, 2018

Businesses: Positive Property Finance / Invisible Investors

Services offered: (1) Property Finance Brokerage. (2) Property Finance Education: Ninja Investor Programme weekend workshop and Recycle Your Cash distance learning programme

Email: kevinwright@thinkpositively.co.uk

Websites: www.positivepropertyfinance.co.uk
www.ninjainvestorprogramme.co.uk
www.recycleyourcash.co.uk

*

Like most kids I dreamed of being a football star, but my first job was at the local council. Then I discovered sales and tried different varieties of sales on for size, but it wasn't until I found financial services that I really got job satisfaction.

So for the last twenty-five years I've enjoyed building relationships with people I can help. Over the past fifteen years, I've been dealing exclusively with property investors. I run two businesses: a brokerage and an education business. My brokerage handles tasks and provides services that every type of property finance investor would need

My interest in property started when my mother bought me a book about property as a birthday present; it was called *Property Renovation Profits.* It's a gift that changed my life. I read the book and I did what it said in the pages. I followed the instructions to a tee: I bought property, renovated it, and sold it for a profit. Then I was fired up enough to do it again. It sounds so simple putting it this way: my mum bought me a book and I took action. That really changed the direction of my life.

The first property I bought was just a house that needed doing up. It was a Victorian semi, and it was in poor condition. I organised people doing the work, added value, and then I sold it for a profit. I took it all in my stride. Although it wasn't particularly easy, it was achievable. I went to a bank to get the financing – you could do that in those days!

When I ran out of money for investing, I took a break for a while. I've never been full-time in property investing and I never intend to be; I'm a broker and I'm an educator. That's what I'm best at.

I've been running my education business for the last five years. I teach people how to finance their properties creatively (as in not simply going to the bank or mainstream mortgage lender looking for financing). These are live weekend workshops known as the Ninja Investor Programme. Alongside this there is the Recycle Your Cash distance learning programme, available as audio or video material.

One of the benefits people get by participating in the Ninja Investor Programme is that they get to redefine how they finance buying a property. They tend to think that buying property requires you to put 25% down, borrow the rest on a mortgage, and then wait a standard six months to try and arrange refinance in order to get as much of your deposit out as you can. That's the way most investors do things, and while it works for some, there are limitations to this approach.

- You're limited to the types of property you buy because they have to be in a fairly mortgageable position.
- You're limited as to the value of property you can buy because you can only buy what you can afford to put 25% down on.
- You're limited in the timeframe because you can only progress as quickly as a mortgage company can process the application.

I teach people that you can buy property without being reliant on mortgages, which means you don't need to put 25% down if you know how. You can complete the transaction much faster—in as quickly as twenty-eight days or less—no matter what the condition of the property you want to purchase.

With creative financing, you have no restriction on the type of property you buy. You can put less cash down in order to buy it and get your cash out much faster.

People learn that getting other people's money for deals as a joint venture, which involves finding someone with a bit of cash and offering them 50% of the profit, is not the most profitable approach. There are ways to fund your investment without giving 50% of your profits away.

If you are going to get other people's money, you need to keep on the right side of an FDA directive that governs who you can and can't get money from for your property, as well as who you can and can't market to.

I teach different ways to find property that's very much out-of-the-box thinking in comparison with the traditional viewpoint on obtaining financing and using traditional mortgages. My Ninja Investors learn how to negotiate with agents and vendors so that the agents are begging you to view their properties.

When it comes to refinancing, I teach people how to get the maximum refinance value on their property. Generally speaking, people tend to get a property down-valued initially and they put more cash into it to lift the value, then they remortgage and draw down the money for the next project. So I teach people some different ways to buy property in terms of speed, the percentage of loans, and that sort of thing.

I've written two books; due for publication early in 2018. I'm just putting the finishing touches to both of them. One is a book that comes straight from the workshop and offers the same content as the workshop, but in the form of a book. The other one details how I used my mindset to deal with cancer last year. It was quite a journey, and I can't say that it was a very enjoyable one. Essentially, I used my mind to beat cancer in eight weeks.

I've been practising neuro-linguistic programming (NLP) for over fifteen years. Therefore, when I received a cancer diagnosis from my doctor, I knew pretty much what I needed to do, which was to use my mind to allow my body to heal itself. I took some chemo as well, but I conditioned my mind so that I wouldn't suffer any adverse effects from chemotherapy. I felt perfectly healthy throughout the whole process—I never even needed to take a single day off work.

I got scanned at different points; I got scanned before chemo and after three treatments. Eight weeks later, I'd reduced it by 90%, and in another twelve weeks I'd got rid of 99%. I've been clear since the end of this year.

I was using NLP and meditating every day throughout this time. I employed both of these techniques, and utilised visualisations to reframe what a cancer diagnosis meant to me. What was the meaning of it, for example? And I worked to turn a negative into a positive. I examined difficult questions, such as why getting diagnosed with cancer was actually a great opportunity. As a result, I was able to carry on working throughout that whole time.

Has that experience changed me as a person? For me, it was just another exercise that proved that NLP works. I got the result I expected to get. In my workshops, I teach people to change the mindsets that they've got. They come in thinking like a mortgage buyer, because if you're dependent on mortgages to buy a property that's how you think.

However, there's actually a more empowering mindset to have, and that's the mindset of a cash buyer. Everyone knows how to think like a cash buyer because we've all bought things for cash, except people don't necessarily use it in property because the numbers are high compared to the cash you have access to.

I teach my workshop participants how to use NLP techniques such as modeling. This shows the participants how to model and behave as a cash buyer and how to use creative finance to give them the ability to go toe-to-toe with cash buyers. This all works out to be more advantageous than people with the mortgage buyer mindset. So, looking back on it, what I achieved with cancer gave me greater authority to talk to people about mindset.

NLP and mindset are very important to me. My first awareness of NLP and mindset came from part of my personal development during the mid-1980s. Most of that came through books; I didn't go to any particular event, but I did read two of Tony Robbins' books when they came out in the eighties. Then I read more than one hundred other books on subjects relating to personal development. I started reading books on NLP roughly ten years later, and I worked with a one-on-one coach between 2000 and 2008.

Unfortunately, most people do nothing with the information that they pay to learn. It's a sad fact of life, but true. The majority of people pay to learn stuff and just put it on the shelf and don't do anything with it. But for those that do take action and implement their new-found knowledge, they often buy properties that they wouldn't have ever dreamed of, or considered buying before. They tend to buy them and get into bigger deals than they thought they were able to.

Along the way in my journey, there have been plenty of challenges such as government regulatory changes. The credit crunch was a true challenge because it changed how most property investors had to work. The method they had been using to buy property didn't work any more. I had a very successful brokerage that virtually stopped working overnight because the lenders stopped lending. Many mortgage brokers left and took up another career, but I chose not to. I just researched and investigated what other ways there could be to finance property in order to replicate what investors were using previously—a legitimate alternative which could work post-credit crunch—and that's what I've been teaching ever since.

Even when things have been really challenging, I've always taken away the positives and found lessons in them. I'm always learning. There's a saying that has become a personal and professional mantra for me: quitters never win and winners never quit. So, I've just applied that to my business and to my personal mindset. When you're having a tough time, just keep going.

One of the biggest lessons that I've learned which has stuck with me long-term, aside from NLP and positive thinking, is that perseverance will overcome almost any objective or obstacle.

My biggest success or achievement that I'm proudest of is having the ability to motivate other people to go out and be successful. That's what I love doing.

There's an annual event, The Property Investor Awards, and at this event, they give out awards in various categories such as New Property Investor of the Year and Deal of the Year and I'm on the judging panel for it. I was a judge in 2015 and 2016 and I'm a judge this year as well.

As a judge, I'm looking for qualities that are relevant to achievement in a particular category. So, if the category is New Investor of the Year—someone fresh into the property business—what have they achieved? If it's the HMO Deal of the Year, do you know what they have achieved in terms of producing their profitable HMO? If it's Development of the Year, what have they achieved in producing a profitable development? There are about eight to ten different categories, and it's very interesting to see what new investors do and what kinds of strategies they follow.

I'm also a speaker and on the speaking circuit regularly. Since 2011, I've probably spoken at a majority of the property meetings in the country. I do less of that now and more speaking at my own one-day events. I occasionally do some speaking for other people's mastermind groups, where you've got people committed on a higher level who are paying a few thousand pounds for a mastermind experience.

I like to work with all kinds of investors. I'll work with experienced, sophisticated investors as well as people who are just starting to invest in property, the whole range—I don't discriminate. What I teach applies to people regardless of where they are in their property journey.

When it comes to my competitors, I offer a different service from what other brokers are offering: I don't know any of them who offer training. Most people just offer the brokerage, but not the necessary training. The training adds to the brokerage services as it gives investors a deeper understanding of what their potential is.

It certainly expands their horizons, you can count on that. You're always going to be limited by whatever amount of cash you've got available, but you can make it stretch further. With the right knowledge you can certainly raise the bar.

My advice to anyone else wanting to invest in property, or thinking of taking the first step, is to do plenty of research and don't be in too much of a hurry to take action before you have had some training. Do your due diligence and find a mentor or a coach. Or come to a property event where you'll meet other like-minded people who can help you and give you guidance.

TINA WALSH

I left the police force in 1995; I was pensioned out after I was injured on duty.

Amazon No1 best-selling author of: *Property Sourcing Compliance: Keeping You on the Right Side of the Law* (available on Amazon).

Business: Sanctuary Property Sourcing Ltd

Email: tina@spsuk.co.uk

Mobile: 07929 205 006

Office: 01200 441802

Website: www.spuk.co.uk

My childhood was happy and settled, and in the main I thought school was great. There was myself and my sister, who was seven years younger than me. Mum and Dad both worked, Mum in a local bakery and Dad at the local power station. At school I loved English language and literature as well as geography, and human biology. Looking back, I did okay in school, but I could have studied harder. I always thought that I was pushing myself, but in reality, I wasn't.

I used to play out an awful lot. I always remember the summers being warmer than they are now, but perhaps that's just me looking back through childhood eyes. I used to have hours of great fun playing out on my bike or running around and playing games, and then when I was about fifteen years old, a group of us started youth hostelling: we used to cycle to youth hostels in the Yorkshire Dales or on the edge of the Lake District. We would stay for a few days, go walking, and just generally have lots of fun. I remember we used to carry all of our food in our rucksacks on our back whilst walking up mountains such as Scafell Pike, Helvellyn and the Old Man of Coniston. We used to love doing that. I've always really loved the countryside, and throughout my childhood spent many hours there, so consider myself to be very lucky.

During my childhood, I had a dream of wanting to become a journalist, and that's why I loved English. My old English teacher at the time, who remains my favourite teacher, said that I needed to study the English language very, very hard, and I obliged. I managed a B in English Language at O Level, which I was pleased with, and a B in English literature, which I had to study for during lunch and after school.

This dream of pursuing journalism changed when a police sergeant friend of my parents came round to the house in uniform. To be quite honest, I rather liked the uniform. Shortly after, a friend of mine (who also joined the police cadets a year ahead of me) attended a school reunion that I was at helping out at. I saw her in her uniform too, and that was it: I had to have that uniform!

At the time, I was 16 and doing my O Levels when I had this new police cadet dream. I also considered the army, my mum had always wanted me to become a nurse, so I applied for the police force, the army, and nursing, having plans B and C in place just as my parents wanted. For them, it was more important to have contingency plans than to focus all of my energy on one objective. I applied for the police cadets despite there being only twelve places for girls in Lancashire available out of three thousand applicants. I was incredibly proud of achieving one of those twelve spots. I don't think I realised at the time exactly how much I had achieved by reaching that goal. There were days in the cadets when I wished I hadn't been one of the twelve girls chosen, but that's another story.

I also have always loved horses as and I imagined one day being a mounted police officer, but because I already had a horse and could already ride, they wouldn't take me on board. Unfortunately, I never achieved that goal.

My very first job before this was when I was 14 at high school. I worked in a local fruit and vegetable shop in the town where I grew up, on a Thursday and a Friday after school and a Saturday half day. I would get off the school bus, go to the shop, and put on my heavy, beige-coloured apron, which was almost like a hessian sack that had been adapted for use—it had to be hardy for handling all the sacks of vegetables and everything. I helped serve customers, lug sacks of vegetables down from the loft, and generally kept the shop clean and tidy after closing.

I always remember the two other girls who used to work with me; they were older than I was and they used to make me get the banana box because they wanted me to take care of the multi-coloured spiders that would occasionally come with the bananas. I was terrified of spiders back then, but because I was the youngest, they used to push me to get the banana boxes. I remember we used to pick the bananas up with two pairs of gloves on, dangle them, and rotate them to see if there were any spiders on them. Some of the spiders were really quite big, so we didn't know if they were poisonous.

As an old-fashioned fruit and vegetable shop, we used to leave the front door open at all times, so in winter it was absolutely freezing. There was really nowhere to go to get warm, with only one Calor gas heater in the back room and the owner, Gordon, would get comfy in front of the heater, and fall asleep on potato sacks whilst we were serving customers in the shop. Overall, I did enjoy my first job at the fruit and vegetable shop and I was earning money, which was great; although I did gave it up eventually because it was just so cold in winter.

Straight after finishing school, I joined the police cadets and spent ten months training at Hutton Hall, which is the training centre for the Lancashire Police Force and next door to the police headquarters for the Lancashire Constabulary, not too far from Preston. From there, I went out at Blackburn Police Station as a cadet until I turned eighteen and a half, at which point I was 'made up' to the rank of woman police constable and given a collar number and a fully-fledged policewoman's uniform.

I then had to attend the national training centre for police forces, Bruche Police Training Centre in Warrington. It's gone now, demolished to make way for a housing estate some years ago, but it was the old training centre for a lot of the local forces. We were there for about ten weeks until we came back to do various levels of courses at headquarters for driving along with other bits and pieces before we eventually went out to section working.

I thought working as a policewoman was fabulous; I loved it. I always wanted a job that when you went into work you didn't know what would happen that day. A few of my friends went into jobs at a local factory near us where they packaged crisps into boxes. Obviously, if packaging crisps is what you want to do and you are very happy doing that, fantastic, but it wouldn't have been for me. I couldn't have stood there putting bags of crisps in boxes day in and day out; it would have driven me nuts. Instead, I went to work and didn't know what I was going to face on any given day.

My first posting as a policewoman was on 17th of December 1979. On my first set of nights, there was a murder. It was Christmas Eve and the husband hadn't come home for Christmas lunch, so she went up to the pub with a pair of scissors that she'd been using and stuck them in him. Not coming home for Christmas lunch was the straw that broke the camel's back—she'd had enough. I spent the night sitting on suicide watch outside the cell where we held the prisoners. So I was thrown in at the deep end.

I was on the police force for just over fourteen years. I had a period of time out when I had my daughter and then applied to go back in again, staying on as a policewoman. I didn't want to rise through the ranks; I wanted to do the job on the ground. I specialised in interviewing and working with social services for abused and sexually abused children and rape victims.

When I joined, there were very few policewomen. There were no mobile phones back then, so because there were very few of us, we had to be on call to cover if they had a woman prisoner in. If it was your turn to be on call, you had to give the office an address and telephone number where you could be reached. We couldn't drink alcohol for obvious reasons, and we couldn't go out because most places didn't have telephones.

I became interested in property during my second marriage. My husband, Tony, and I have always loved property, and we were always driving around the area looking for potential houses and buildings that could be converted or land that could be built on. We didn't necessarily have the money to be able to do that, apart from the property that we were living in, but we were always really interested. We monitored the housing market and the prices.

We used the housing market to move up the property ladder ourselves: we would buy something that needed a lot of work done, do the work on it whilst we were living in it, then sell and move on to the next project.

In 2005, we decided to take it a step further and move into property investment. It was something that we'd thought was a good idea, and it was—on paper. We purchased two, brand-new off-plan properties from a builder, making every rooky mistake in the book. We didn't know—there were no training courses. Later that year, there was a delay on the build and then the crash happened in 2007, so we ended up losing faith in property investment.

We couldn't sell the properties immediately because we would have suffered a loss, so we ended up having to move into one. We rented out the other one for a short period of time and finally managed to sell it on. We learned a hard lesson, and it put us off investing. There was no one to teach us what to do, and whilst having extra money coming in from an investment property and gaining increasingly valuable property were great ideas, they didn't work for us at that time, because we invested poorly.

We ended up living in that property for ten years because at the point in time when we could sell it, the children were growing up and they were at high school. Most of their friends lived in that neighbourhood and the school bus stopped right outside the house, so it didn't make sense to suddenly move them. They were settled, but it did put our plans on hold.

I left the police force in 1995; I was pensioned out after I was injured on duty. It was in the early summer, and I was called to an incident at a pub in Burnley where I was working. We went into the pub and the landlady told us that a young girl had put her fist through the Victorian glass window in one of the original pub doors. The landlady came outside with me and pointed out who the girl was; I went over and told the girl that she was under arrest, and she went bananas.

Back then, I was considerably slimmer and she was a rather large girl of sixteen. She bounced me from pillar to post, but I didn't let go of her. I shouted for assistance via my radio, which took a little while to arrive.

That evening, when I was taking statements regarding the damage, I lost the use of my right hand. I had to wiggle my fingers around and get hold of the pen to start writing again, but it kept happening. I thought I'd just banged my arm—I didn't think anything of it—but a few days later, I was getting horrendous shooting pains through my arm, down into my fingers, and up into my shoulder and my neck. I went to the doctor he prescribed cream to apply, some tablets, and finally some physiotherapy treatment, but nothing worked. I didn't work during this time because I didn't want the damage to get any worse, and I had to go to a nerve specialist for all sorts of tests. They said the nerve damage was permanent. I'm now classed as being partially disabled (17% I think), though I don't like to make a big deal of it.

My arm doesn't stop me from doing anything; it does, however, let me know when I've done too much. Occasionally I will pick something up and forget, and whatever I'm carrying will drop. My brain doesn't tell me it's going to do it, so I have to be careful when I'm getting something hot out of the oven. Driving long distances can hurt, but I've learned to adapt. It's there, it hurts most of the time—it's like having a toothache in your elbow joint, but it could have been a lot worse.

Because of this injury, the police force pensioned me out. Back then if you couldn't work as a front-line police officer, you were pensioned out. I was devastated because I really didn't want to leave—that was never the plan.

I felt sorry for myself for a while until Tony literally took me to the Job Centre. He parked the car outside and made me get out and go in. I got a little job managing a tile shop in Clitheroe, and I ended up spending quite a few years doing that—learning all about tiles, the differences in types of tiles and how they're manufactured. I really loved it. I also went back to college to learn how to develop and build databases for project management. I went on to be a PA for a children's speech and language therapist, and then moved on to project manage a new school build for a local school. For six years, I ran their £10 million new school appeal for raising money to pay their percentage of the build costs. During that time, I built the database, managed and sent out the letters, and managed the cash going into the appeal bank account.

From that point, I accidentally fell into healthcare. My sister-in-law was running a healthcare business, and she'd always asked me to go on board with her and I'd said, "*No, I don't want to wipe people's bottoms.*" But one day I got a telephone call with news that she'd had to sack the manager. She asked if I would go in and help with the systems. Of course I ended up staying, becoming a full-time employee and gaining my NVQ 4 in Leadership and Management in Care, eventually rising to become the company operations manager.

My sister-in-law's healthcare business was eventually sold, but we both stayed with the company, transferring across with all of our staff, saying that we would give it six months to see how it went. It didn't go very well, and my sister-in-law ended up leaving before I did; as a senior manager, I had to give six months' notice.

The team that I had worked with to develop the management and rostering software for the company found out that I was leaving and asked me if I would work with them to help develop the software further, and carry out demonstrations and training for them on their systems. I had the database development and systems background, but I also had a great understanding of the healthcare sector as well.

About two-and-a-half years later, my sister-in-law, who had sold the healthcare business, asked me to work with her again, this time helping healthcare companies find buyers and sell their businesses. She asked me if I wanted to get on board and help to source the healthcare businesses. So for a while I worked with both my sister-in-law and the software training company.

In the beginning, the sourcing of healthcare businesses seemed to gel quite well with the sourcing of properties for our clients, but then over time it started to take me away from home far too much. So much so, that I decided to drop the sourcing of healthcare businesses completely and fully focus on developing a business for us both to be involved in. Tony and I had been talking about doing this for some time with a goal to have it running for when he retired, we knew that we wanted it to be property related, but were unsure as to exactly what are we would focus on. Until a mentor asked if we knew what 'property sourcing' was.

I was introduced to the idea of mentors and training when I was dragged kicking and screaming to a three-day event at the ExCel Centre in London. My good friend, Sarah, brought me along because her husband wouldn't attend; she wanted to see Tony Robbins.

We listened to a variety of speakers, but there was one who stood out: his name is Kevin Green. Originally a farmer from Wales, he told us the story of how he got into property: how he was fed up and he didn't want to take over the family farm, he applied for and won a scholarship to go around various countries to interview entrepreneurs to find out what set them apart from everyone. He eventually ended up on Sir Richard Branson's doorstep, who became his mentor.

Kevin seemed a really down-to-earth guy. I was really enamoured with the fact that he was the only speaker over the three days that had spoken about property, which was already an interest for Tony and me.

I spoke to Tony about it when I got home, but it took me six months to persuade him to actually go and listen to Kevin speak. Finally, in December 2011, we both attended one of Kevin's events in Manchester. At the end of it, Tony was just as impressed as I had been and because we really wanted to develop the business before Tony retired, we decided to sign up with Kevin's mentorship programme.

A month later, in January 2012, we sat down with Kevin and our personal coach Daniel Latto and just chatted. They got to know us: what our likes and dislikes were, what we were keen on, what we loved doing, and they asked us if we had considered property sourcing. We asked what that was and we were told to go and research it. And that was how my property sourcing and compliance journey started.

The thought of starting a new business absolutely terrified me. At that point, I would rather have donned my police uniform and gone out and faced the guy who pointed a sawn-off shotgun at me some years before; I was completely outside my comfort zone preparing to run our own business. I'd been self-employed for some time, but worked alongside other people, which isn't the same as running a business for yourself—setting up a business was completely alien to me.

However, I also like a challenge, and I never give in or give up. In fact, the term 'give up' is not in my vocabulary at all. So, I did the research, perhaps because of my police background when we had to learn law verbatim, I found it easy enough to read and understand but of course at that time there were no property sourcing courses to help, so it was all down to me.

We spent close to a year researching and crewing for Kevin on his events because we knew that investors who had a lot of money, but not much time, would also be attending. The north of England was becoming a popular place to invest for people from further south. They had cash, but obviously needed someone to support them. And that was how the business started. We linked up with investors from crewing at Kevin's events, used my recently-acquired knowledge, crossed our fingers, and ran with it to see how it worked out.

It took us thirteen months from that January to actually get our first cheque payment for the first sourcing deal. I scanned it and printed it and we still have it. It was a fantastic feeling. It felt an awful long time coming, but we learned a lot on the journey as well.

Now we just had to wash, wipe, and repeat, find more investors interested in investing and find more properties to source—that's basically what we do.

An unexpected door that re-opened was from my previous links to the healthcare sector. There are many healthcare companies that look for development sites or properties, and a few of them got in touch with me regarding those services. Things moved from looking for the two-bedroom terraced houses for the buy-to-let market to the small HMOs looking for up to 40-acre development sites or blocks of flats for the healthcare sector. I had to learn how to assess a development site, which is completely different from the process for a two-bedroom terraced house for buy-to-let.

I was very lucky that an old school local builder contacted me and asked for a meeting on LinkedIn. He took me around the sites he owned and gave me first option on them. Along with a good friend, Mark Stokes-Denson, he talked me through how it worked, and that was how I learned.

I think that my interest in property sourcing compliance stems from having been a police officer and wanting everything done legally. The first thing that I looked into when Kevin told us to research property sourcing was the legalities of it. How did it have to be set up to be legal? Were there any laws that governed it? It took longer for me to set up the company by focusing on complying with the regulations because a lot of sourcers just start sourcing—they don't necessarily set up the structures that we have.

Many property sourcers don't follow the law. It was interesting when investors were coming to me and saying, '*Do you have any deals, Tina*?' and I would turn round and say, '*Well actually, I don't work like that.*' Here's the way that I work: investors come on board with me and I take time to learn what their investment strategies are, what they want to do, and where they want to do that. They go through a registration process with me and then I source to order for that specific investor. Many other sourcers find a deal and then launch it out to the wider market. I've never worked that way, probably because I started by crewing for Kevin and we found the investors before we started looking for the properties. I wanted a buyer there ready to buy, not a property that I didn't know if I would find a buyer for. That was just the way that my brain worked.

We've always worked in this way: we source to order for our investors who come through the registration process. But the bottom line is that it doesn't matter whether you source deals first or investors to buy them, as long as you do it compliantly.

Today, we have three business areas: property sourcing (the original business), a company where we invest personally in property and my book and training and consultation around property sourcing compliance. We have finally dipped our toes back in the property investment sector again and we have purchased a block of six flats on the Fylde Coast that we are refurbishing and then will either flip or re-finance and hold.

My ultimate goal for the compliance side of the business is to raise standards across the industry by educating investors as to how to spot a non-compliant sourcer so that they aren't taken for a ride by unscrupulous and illegal sourcers. At the same time, I also want to raise standards for property sourcing and, if necessary, reduce the amount of property sourcers and have the majority of them 100-percent compliant so that we raise the perception of the industry.

I think my biggest aha moment with regard to property was when we first received that cheque, our first ever fee. It was in my hand and I realised that not only could I do it, but that it did work, and all I had to do then was to increase what we were doing and the business would work very well.

My best advice to others is to never give up. Do something that you love, don't do something because you think it's going to make you money – because at the end of the day, it won't if you don't love it. You have to love something; you have to be passionate about it. If there's a problem that you face, there's always a way round it, under it, over it, or through it. It's never an impossible task; there's always a way of doing something. I think I've always been like that, probably from being a police officer for so long. Just never give in. If it's what you really want to do, don't listen to the naysayers and don't listen to people saying you can't do that or you'll never do that. Yes, you will, but you have to focus on it, and you have to take steps every day to achieve it and never lose sight of the goal. Don't let anyone put you off.

I think I have been pushing past my comfort zone for the last twelve months, certainly. If you're entrepreneurial-spirited, you're constantly pushing those barriers and expanding your comfort zone. But for the last 12 months, between writing my book and moving back into personal reinvesting, During times like that I do sometimes suffer from anxiety attacks, I think because we're pushing the boundaries again.

I believe a great deal in mind set. If you focus on negatives, you get a lot more negatives. If you focus on positives, you see a lot more positives. When you're pushing your comfort zone, your mind has a habit of tagging onto, '*What if this happens? What if that happens? Oh my goodness, if that happens, this will happen and that will happen,*' and before you know it, you're spiralling down this negativity into utter despair. When an anxiety attack kicks in you can feel it in your chest like a great weight pressing down on you, but I always say to myself, '*Are you in immediate danger? Are you in danger of something horrible happening to you today or tomorrow or this week?*' And that usually brings the anxiety levels gradually down because I'm bringing myself back down to reality.

Besides my husband and children, writing my book *Property Sourcing Compliance* and publishing it has to be my biggest achievement. It had been in my head for three years. I'd started it, but I hadn't had a clue when I started it how on earth I was going to publish it, or how to write a book, but I made a start and I started writing it. It's taking that step—starting something and then asking for help when you get to the point where you don't know what to do next. The book has led to many speaking opportunities.

Speaking has opened doors for me. It has brought to the fore the fact that there are actually compliance issues around property sourcing which no one else is speaking about. I have been offered opportunities to speak about what I'm passionate about now – compliance – along with the development of the courses and consultations. But what's amazing, more than anything else, is that when I was crewing for Kevin I was seeing everyone in the coffee breaks flocking around him to speak to him. I remember thinking to myself, '*that would be wonderful if one day I could do that, if I could give something back and people would flock around me in that way as they do with other leading lights in our industry.*'

At the end of the last couple of presentations that I have done, there was applause, and that was fantastic. Then, I went and sat at the desk to dismantle my laptop. When I looked up, the desk was surrounded by people wanting to ask me questions—that was one of those surreal moments. They actually wanted to ask me questions. When I'm standing up in front of them, it's where I want to be. It's a huge passion, and I love doing it. I love supporting people and passing on my knowledge. My passion for compliance and raising standards will always be there, but I now know that presenting and working with people to pass on my knowledge is also up there with it. I love what I do.

DAVID HUMPHREYS

July 1969: Armstrong makes his "Giant Leap for Mankind" on the Moon. August 1969: I make my Giant Leap opening a Letting Agency in Oxford.

Serial property investor and developer with over 40 years' experience. Author of 'Investing in Residential Property'. Founder of The Property Auction Expert Programme.

Business: Property Investor Online

Services offered: Consultancy. Armchair acquisition. Investment education. Mastermind Classes. One-to-one mentoring.

Tel: 07970 028539

Websites: www.propertyinvestoronline.com
   www.buyingauctionproperty.com
   www.propertyauctionexpert.com

*

I grew up on a mixed farm where we raised livestock and grew crops like barley and sugar beet. My father was a farmer and later became a breeder in the UK, specialising in turkeys, but my childhood was spent on a mixed farm. I started working on the farm when I was about 14 during school holidays, and kept doing that until I was 19 when I took off to Canada. I emigrated to Canada to get away because I wasn't very good at school as I didn't particularly like it. Being threatened with the prospect of Agricultural College, I hightailed it out of there and left for Canada where I was supposed to go farming, but I had no intention of that. I got on a boat in Liverpool and got off a week later knowing nobody.

In those days, if you wanted to communicate, mail took 10 days from Canada, and you had to book a phone call, so it was quite different from today. First of all, I started working in a department store in Toronto selling snow blowers, and up until that point I had never seen one before in my entire life. But I was quite good at that. I soon found out that they were going to dismiss me after they'd done a stock check at the beginning of the New Year. So, I resigned straight away and went to Montreal, where they had just had a heavy snowstorm and I spent a week shovelling snow on the streets but couldn't find work because I didn't speak French.

Snow cleared, I headed back to Toronto and worked in a carwash for some weeks. Early in the New Year, I started selling Encyclopaedia Britannica . I also did the stereotypical lumbering job where I spent a month working in the Rockies, crossing Canada by train and bus. For my 21st birthday, I came back to England, and ended up working in an advertising agency in London.

From 1962, onwards I spent about six or seven years in various marketing positions, always intending to head back to Canada. There seemed to always be somebody asking me to come and work with them, so I'd cancel going back to Canada and starting over. Finally, I was headhunted into a London letting agency, called Central Flats. All we did was let flats or bedsits in Earls Court, Gloucester Road and Beauchamp Place. No management or anything like that, just lettings. That went on for a couple of years and it was quite good fun. Then I reached the defining moment.

The guy who owned the letting agency had this fantastic idea that he wanted me to work on, so we worked on it for a couple of months but didn't get anywhere, and I said to him, "Look, you know, this isn't working out, I'll go back and carry on with the letting agency, and keep everybody there happy." But he turned around and said, "Look, I sign the cheques, you do as you're told." So I said, "Yeah, I can see that. You sign the cheques, I should do as I'm told." I quit. At this point in time, I was married with a little baby and thought, "If I don't quit now – with the child and everything else – I will gradually reach a point where I can't quit and have too many responsibilities." So, I resigned and moved to Oxford (I came from Oxford originally as the farm was outside the city). I rented a flat in Headington, and started a letting agency in Oxford in 1969. We opened up just after Armstrong had landed on the moon.

It was quite a simple business really. We charged the person who was looking for the flat or bedsit or whatever a week's rent as a fee, and offered a free service to landlords. When we started off, if a person came into the office and we didn't have anything suitable, we did various things. We would tell them where to go, the streets, and if they found something they didn't like, to call us about it and we'd give them 10 shillings (50p today) and phone the landlord with our free service. That's how it all started, and I've been in property ever since.

The defining moment for me was my understanding that you are either going to be in control or you're not. The problem is that so many people can't leave their work because they've got too many commitments, with schools, etc. If they leave their job to go out on their own, with just a wife and a baby, they can mostly get away with it. In my case, if I had had two or three kids and a mortgage and everything else, I couldn't have done it. It was literally a £25 start-up. People said I was mad; I know it sounds mad in retrospect. My wife's parents had similar thoughts: "If you're mad, we're not going to help you. You're going to get into trouble, and don't expect to come running to us. We won't help you at all. Stay where you are."

I got into auctions fairly early. I knew what auctions were about having first attended them as a kid with my father when he bought and sold sheep and cattle at auctions. Back in about '96 or so, I went to an auction and bought a property and really enjoyed it. I always liked the auction game. By this time, I was running quite a big letting and managing agency in Oxford, and people were saying, "Come and do it for me. Buy the property, fix it up and let it." So I did. Then I started to look elsewhere, at places like County Durham and Wandsworth, London, to see what was going on. I ended up finding properties – we're now going back to '98, '99 – in some places that were very, very cheap. You could go up into the north, County Durham, for example, and buy a property for £25,000 at auction which was returning over 20% yield. It made sense to do that: you'd just buy the cash return.

So, we started going to auctions in earnest, employing various methods and analysis to help us on our way. So, for example, if a remodelled property is worth £100,000, fix it up for about £30,000, add another £3,000 to 5,000 for costs of buying it, etc., and add in a bit of profit, then if you could buy the property for around £50,000, or less, it works. That's the methodology: work back from the fixed-up value.

We started off, as most people do, doing 'makeovers' as I call them, where you just redecorate, put in a new bathroom and kitchen and fix minor repairs, something along those lines. This was a mad time back in the late '90s, early 2000s. In those days, loads of people were typically after properties that needed work. Mad to the degree that if you found a property that was in good order, you made it need work. Now, you went down the local tip and got an old bath (avocado), put it in to replace the decent bath, made the property nice and dirty, boarded it up, and you could made money overnight. It would go for more than you'd pay for the decent house. I remember going to see one property, which was a little back-to-back terraced house in Stockport. You had to walk carefully across the front garden just to get into the house. The front garden was a rubbish tip about 15 or 20 feet across. And because it needed fixing up, 90 people came to view the house over two days.

The braver you are, the more you make, so if you only go into properties that just need some decorating, and minor repairs don't expect to make any money out of it: redecs really don't add value, they just speed up the sale. But if you find a property which still has the loo outside, it will be a different story. I bought a house once where the work-surface in the kitchen was quite low – when I lifted it up, I found a plumbed in bath underneath; the work-surface was even slotted at the end to allow for the bath taps. And this wasn't that long ago: about 2005 or 2006. The loo was in a corner and, for privacy, was behind a curtain. But seriously, the kitchen-work surface was just a length of work-surface sitting on top of the bath!

What makes it fun is when this type of property goes through the auction process: you've got 15 minutes to look at an auction property and decide what you're going to do. You can go back a number of times, three maybe four, but within any viewing day it's all 15-minute viewing slots. It doesn't matter whether it's a two-bedroom terraced house, a one-bedroom flat, or a big property of five or six bedrooms, it's still 15 minutes when you get into areas like County Durham and South Wales. In London, it's a bit longer: they double the time. You have 30 minutes to get around a London property and decide what you're going to do with it.

The most profitable properties are those where you've got to go back to bare walls, floors and lath and plaster ceilings and start from scratch. In south Wales, I was spending £25,000 – £30,000 fixing up a property which I'd only paid £25,000 – £30,000 for. But having fixed it up, it was probably worth £85,000 – £95,000, which meant I could re-mortgage it, get all my money out and start again. This is basically the strategy we teach today, a cookie-cutter, on buying at auction and how you get into it.

Teaching buying at auction grew out of a lecture I did in 2012, when I was teaching tax-free rent and no money left in. Tax-free rent results from the work you do. But I was saying to a group of about 20 people in the lecture that the place to start to do this is buying at auction, because you are provided with a constant supply of properties that need work. If you go to a busy auction, like the Birmingham one we work out of, then you can see 20 or 30 suitable properties over a couple of days. Now, the list will winnow down after you do the due diligence, check the legal pack and cost the fix-up, to maybe two, three, or four that you are actually thinking about bidding on in the auction room. It's a numbers game, and you've got to do the numbers to find the deals.

Interestingly enough, provided a property is habitable and you can technically mortgage it – and this house that I spoke of, where the kitchen had its work-surface on the bath, was habitable, and people were living in it, or had been recently, it had a loo, had water connected, had electricity connected and a working kitchen. The fact that there was a bath in the kitchen didn't matter.

That property needed stripping back to bare walls and bare floors. If you find these types of properties and pay £25,000 – £30,000 for them – they're still available at that price today – and fix them up, you can claim anything you fix up that didn't exist before as a repair for tax purposes. So, for example, the new kitchen where a kitchen existed before: everything in that is a repair, unless you increase the number of units when it all becomes a capital cost. The new bathroom where a bathroom already existed is a repair. A lot of these properties needed new roofs because they were so dilapidated, so if you go in and put a new roof on, that's a repair. If you go to places like Wales and the north, an up-and-over roof on a terraced house will today cost you about £5,000. That means that you've got to make £5,000 taxable profit from rent before you start paying tax.

So, if you've spent £30,000 fixing a property, about 70% gets classified as a repair and you've got quite a long time before you start running into paying tax. Hence, you've got this sort of tax-free situation, but the only thing about it is that if the Inland Revenue, HMRC, decides that your roof isn't a repair, but is a capital cost, then when you sell the property you put the cost of the roof against your capital gains before tax. Either way, you get a tax break on the work done. And there are some real anomalies to it. If you take a property with single-glazed metal-framed windows and you replace all the windows with double- or triple-glazed UPVC, you'd call that an improvement. But the taxman in his wisdom will declare, "No, it's a repair, because you're using modern technology." A quick way of identifying suitable property worth spending due diligence time on is look for property with an EPC rating below 55.

These are the sorts of topics I lecture on, which gave rise to the students back in 2012 saying, "Yeah, but we don't know anything about auctions. Can you help us on that?" In response, I told them I'd put together an auction course, and I did, a Masterclass that ran for the first time in February 2013. The main thing that we do now is talk about auctions, and also about tax-free rent. No Money Left In – that comes around by taking your £30,000 property, spending £30,000 on it, and then going out and re-mortgaging it for £60,000. So, you draw your money out, because it's worth £85,000 – £95,000, and you can then start again. Taking your money out lets you recycle your capital and keep going without being dependent on market-driven growth which you would have to do otherwise.

And the auctions also give you regular reliable supply. To find even half a dozen properties that you can actually fix up could take you months in the estate agents' offices, but at auction they're there, with over 2,000 properties a month available in the auction rooms across the country. There is an auction house in Birmingham we work with that runs an auction of about 140 lots every six to eight weeks, and there is one down in Kent that runs an auction of 80 lots during that same time-frame. Most of these auction properties need work.

Today, as well as property investment, still buying and fixing up run down properties, my time is spent mostly training prospective auctions buyers and in all aspects of finding and buying properties in auctions that work for the buyer's strategy. This training ranges from recorded 1-to-1 online meetings through open-mike webinars to network meeting and pre-auction seminars one-day workshops and the Masterclass which is limited to 12 students. If I'm teaching in a conference room we can take 30, 40 students through a one-day, but we limit the number in a Masterclass to 12 because two days are spent viewing properties with other interested buyers.

Currently, we're looking to build up the training. Two students who've done a Masterclass, want to come on board and run masterclasses themselves, so we're building it up now. Obviously, there have been challenges along the way. For one thing, legislation keeps changing, and in some cases you can't see it coming. The most recent change was Osborne's decision to limit and eventually stop the deduction of mortgage interest from the rent before you pay tax. It's what's called Section 24 on the pay-out side, and that's having a big knock-on effect. Also, the changes in the Stamp Duty rules don't help. For as long as I can remember private property investment and letting has been a political football which seems to be continuing today even with a Conservative Government.

Back in the 1980s, when I was in Oxford, I ran a holiday-letting scheme. The idea was inspired by the long sabbaticals and summer holidays that Oxford University lecturers enjoyed. I noticed that their big houses in the middle of Oxford all stood empty for six weeks, even two months, whilst the owner was away in Tuscany, the States, or wherever else. So, I had the idea of letting these homes to the summer visitors who come to

Oxford for language courses or are what are called, culture vultures. It went well. We ran that for about 10 years, and peaked the year before the Gulf War, when we had 210 beds occupied out of an availability of 230 or so. We were then the biggest "hotel" in Oxford. We used to do a minimum of three-day lets. Our business was doing fine, and we had people coming from all over the world, with a lot out of the Middle East, the States, and other long-haul starting points. A lot of our families came from Spain, as well, on English-learning holidays. I used to take these families, put them into Oxford family homes, charge them bed and breakfast rates, include a weekly cleaning and bedlinen service and let them enjoy English family life in Oxford for a few weeks, even down to looking after the cat if they were happy to do so.

Then the government in its wisdom decided that fire regulations on furniture had to come in (this was an EU thing), and that you couldn't let a property that didn't have fire resistant furniture. Overnight, the business was dead because these homes in Oxford did not have compliant furniture. Today, you can't buy furniture that's not compliant, but back in the early '90s a lot of properties we dealt with didn't comply.

The next obstacle was always the amount of naysayers who would tell you "Oh, I wouldn't do that, I wouldn't let that, I wouldn't blah, blah, blah," when you were breaking new ground. Working on the holiday homes was a good example, as was spending £30,000 on a £30,000 property. It was just bothersome, the amount of people who would tell you, "you shouldn't be doing it anyway," when you hadn't even asked for their advice.

This was coming from both acquaintances and people at the Council, Planning Departments, Housing Officers, Tourist Boards, etc. We are a very negative nation. I remember many years ago someone telling me a story. The American worker arrives at his workplace and sees his boss driving in a Cadillac and says, "One day I'm gonna own that," and works towards owning his Cadillac. Whereas the British guy turns around and says, "He must have ripped somebody off to get his Cadillac." So it's very difficult. With the holiday homes business, I remember people saying I shouldn't do it. To which I would ask, "Why can't I do it?" Their response would be, "Well, I wouldn't do it." When people say something like that, they don't want you to succeed, or even to try to.

So other people's negativity is probably one of the biggest obstacles. It can come right back into your own home, when you want to do something and in the planning stages someone tells you, "Oh, I don't know about that. I wouldn't do that. That's not been done before, has it?" "Well, no, it hasn't been done before, but does that matter?" "Well, if it hasn't been done before, there must a good reason why it hasn't been done before." In spite of all of this negativity, I kept going from sheer bloody-mindedness. It was just too interesting. I need, and we all need, to be doing something that gets us out of the bed in the morning, excited about what's going to happen through that new day. And time and again, I would literally go to bed and wake up thinking, "Oh, I must get on with this. I must get on with that. That's what I want to do today."

The idea of lying in bed to me is anathema, yet many live that life. There's a neighbour of mine – I don't know him well – who is now retired. I don't know what age he is, maybe 55, 60, if that. And his day now is trudging to a pub, spending his mornings and evenings there, and trudging back. That's no life at all. He doesn't look excited about it; he doesn't look a happy camper. He's grown a beard, looks pretty unkempt, and slouches. The life's gone out of him and he admits to missing his workmates. I want to do something that gets me out of bed in the morning looking forward to the new day, and watching soaps on TV, even Homes Under The Hammer and Martin Roberts, doesn't do it for me.

I had no one to guide me along the way, so it was mostly trial and error: lots of trials, and lots and lots of errors, some of them expensive. Some haven't been so expensive, but the majority have been very expensive. You've got to make mistakes. Once again, if you're afraid of making a mistake, forget it. Stick with the day job, because you only learn by making mistakes. Mistakes really embed themselves in you and then you try and work out how not to make the mistake again. Unfortunately, without a guide or mentor, I've made the same mistake several times, but, there's always been a sort of different take on it. Mistakes don't come cleanly wrapped, they come sort of hazy. You made a mistake. Why? You can't quite pick out why. Why did that go pear-shaped? Yet other times, things are very clear. I remember viewing a house once, walking into it, and for some reason the rear door which led into an attached garage, that was locked. I couldn't get in to see the garage. Anyway, it came to auction and seemed like a good price from what I could see, so I bought it. When I eventually managed to open the back door, I found that the rear wall of the house, was perpendicular inside, but bent like a banana on the other side. I had bought three walls and a roof. It cost me about £10,000 to take the wall down and rebuild it; it was a two feet thick stone wall. An expensive mistake for not checking behind a locked door.

The best advice I would give to somebody else wanting to achieve what I have is: think outside the box. The fact that somebody else has done it doesn't matter. Generally speaking, there is always 'an angle' you can bring to any property. One of the things that I've done involves the 27% of the housing stock in this country that are terraced houses. Provided I've got a footprint of the terraced house 23 feet deep by 12 feet six, 13 feet wide, excluding any kitchen/bathroom extension, and the staircase runs away from the front door parallel to the party walls and not across the middle, I've taken the staircase out and forwards towards the front door, effectively putting part of the hall floor upstairs. I can now build a bathroom upstairs without losing a bedroom, this is a capital cost by the way, not a repair. Now, I came up with that idea about 30 years ago, and all my fix ups work on that basis, a cookie-cutter. By doing that, I've massively improved the property and its value. But once again, people were saying, "Well, you can't take a staircase out. Isn't that structural?" No, it's not. It's just a piece of timber bolted to a wall.

The next important thing is that you must become a real expert in what you do. You need to constantly ask, "What if? What if? What if?" so you become really knowledgeable on whatever you're trying to do. You have to be able to stand up to cross-examination. If you go into training, then you're asked all sorts of questions and need to be able to answer straight away. It's not good enough to say, "Oh, I'll have to think about that. I'll come back to you." That should happen very, very rarely.

When I lecture, most of the time the webinars I run which are open mike so people can interrupt and ask questions – I don't want to wait until the end of a presentation to go into a Q&A session. I want people to ask questions as we roll, because it keeps me on my toes, and also the questions they ask invariably push me. I know that what I know is not because I've conventionally learnt it, but because I've been asked about it. That's the reason I have the knowledge that I do. It isn't from studying books, it's from being asked questions by people interested in what I do.

There's no easy way to do it. Whatever you're going to get into, you need to become a really in-depth expert on your niche subject or topic, whatever it is. You also need to be asking about it all the time, because you never, ever get to the point where you know it all. My advice to anyone getting into anything that they want to do is that it has to be something that you want to get up in the morning and do. Not play golf; you've got to live this. You've got to enjoy it 24/7, literally. Something will crop up during the day, and it soon becomes a toss-up whether you go and do your work or your play. Your work needs to come first and be the major pull. People like Hamilton and Vettel, the F1 drivers, don't jump in cars because they're paid to, they do it because they get off on it even though they are paid millions. They'd rather do that than anything else. Anybody at the peak of what they're doing, would rather do that than anything else. Whenever you try and pay them to do something else, they say, "no". Passion is the biggest thing. You see too many people trudging to work for their life 'after hours'. Their life begins at 6pm or 10pm or at the weekends.

The very first step to take for someone who is interested in property investing is to get in with somebody who is doing it. Go to a network meeting. At most network meetings, you get literally 10 seconds to say who you are and why you're there. So, you stand up and quickly say, "I am... name, etc. I am interested in property and would like to work for free with somebody who is actually doing this. And if you feel that you'd like to have an assistant, I'll pay my own way. I'll come to you. Come and talk to me."

We're now marketing the Auction Masterclass, and I need to get to people who are interested in auctions. If I go into a network meeting and say, "I'm doing auctions, blah, blah, blah," there may be one or two people there who are interested in it, and half a dozen will say, "Oh, no, no. Auctions are too expensive. Auctions are this, auctions are that. You can't buy cheaply at auctions." Well, I'm not trying to buy cheaply. I'm trying to buy property that I can make work. It doesn't have to be cheap. So, we are now going to put on a one-hour seminar before the auction that finishes half an hour before the auction, so we don't interfere with the auction at all, and it's free. You can come in and listen to me during these seminars. I will look at the catalogue, go through it, find the sorts of properties that I think will make money, and put them up along with other tips on how to find the right deals and win the bidding war.

Everyone these days expects to get paid, but in fact, if you are open to volunteering, go to a network meeting and put your hand up and say, "I'd like to work with somebody." There's no obligation. The person you're going to work with isn't obliged to you, nor are you to him. If you pick the right person, there may be a job at the end of it. You'll certainly receive some mentoring and guidance, and you'll see how you fit with them, as well. It's your own personal gain.

I teach people. There are some people who like my style of teaching, while others don't. And do I change for the others? No, because I enjoy the way I do it. So I suggest volunteering with someone who knows what they're doing and has a proven track record. You can watch them. Today on the Internet, you can look at almost anybody on YouTube, see what they do, how they speak, and so forth. But too many people ask, "I'd like to work with you. What will you pay me?" I'm not paying you anything. I'm giving you the opportunity to work with me, free at the coalface, training, and that's good enough.

My biggest success to date that I am most proud of is my business with the holiday homes. I have also spent a lot of time on Excel analysis: I'm sort of known as Mr. Spreadsheet, because I analyse ad-nauseam, right down to the single ingredient. I liken property investment to a fruitcake, a product that has numerous ingredients, with the ingredients interacting with each other to produce a cake. Now, my perfect fruitcake probably would not be your perfect fruitcake – though they can both be absolutely right

– as I don't have a sweet tooth and prefer savoury. You can make a fruitcake of the savoury type, but someone who's got a sweet tooth won't particularly like it.

The same goes for property investment. There are so many facets to it: the mortgage, the location, the neighbourhood, the type of tenant. And you have to decide what you're going to do and how you're going to do it. The principle focus should always be the customer, the tenant, the occupier, and the buyer. Just as a perfect fruitcake doesn't exist, so the perfect property strategy doesn't exist. It's up to you and what you want. My strategy, as an older person, will be very different to the strategy of someone in their thirties, for instance. I want cash and they probably want capital growth, for example. So, what I try to do is break these things down into the tiny components: the single currant, the single spoonful of treacle, the single spoonful of flour or butter. I try to see what happens with one spoonful, or what happens with two. This is how I approach the property analysis game, because there are so many different factors and so many different aims and objectives, and no single right way of doing it. This is what makes it fascinating.

The other thing I'm proud of is my attempt to stay honest – I've tried to cut out the bullshit. Too many in this game talk about becoming a millionaire in a year. Well, the odd person might make it. The odd person wins the pools, the premium bonds, the lottery. But you can't base a strategy on winning the lottery, and you can't go into this game expecting to become a millionaire and be disappointed if you're not. There's a lot of luck in getting to the millionaire level, but you can't base a business solely on that desire. I think what makes the Masterclasses and things like that more interesting is that I go back so far and have seen so many things.

JULIE HANSON

I started my business when my children were young. That sounds crazy, but they were the catalyst that made me do it.

Founder and Managing Director of leading property portal, www.justdoproperty.com.

Mum of two beautiful daughters. Manages a property portfolio and built the Just Do Property with her husband, Alec.

Business: Just Do Property Ltd

Services: We run a website for property investors, offering help and advice for novice and experienced investors

Email: julie@justdoproperty.co.uk

Website: www.justdoproperty.co.uk

*

I grew up in Stockport, near Manchester, which is where I live now (I moved back after a stint in the South!). I lived with my mum and my younger sister; my dad passed away when I was 12. We didn't have much money as Mum supported us with her part-time cleaning job and looked after us at the same time. Despite that, we still had a great childhood. She managed to always give us an annual holiday, which we looked forward to all year!

I actually worked for Hewlett-Packard as my first job; I started working there when I was 16. They used to have what was called a YTS or a Youth Training Scheme (showing my age!).

So, I started off at HP and people said, 'you'll never get a job there; you're too young'. But I was offered two jobs in two years, which I was really pleased about. I absolutely loved working for them. They were a fantastic company.

I also did a degree in Business Administration at Manchester University. I did that on a part-time basis, as well as working full-time. I just worked my way up. I ended up in sales and marketing, which I really enjoyed, but after nearly 20 years of working for them I decided I wanted to run my own business. It had always been in the back of my head. I wanted to have a flexible working environment. At that time, I had my two children—my two lovely daughters—and I just wanted to be able to work around them.

So, I made the decision to give up my corporate life and start my own business.

So, I started my own business when my children were young. That sounds crazy, but they were the catalyst that made me do it. It probably wasn't the best time in terms of time management and things like that, but I did it.

There probably was a defining moment for me when I realised that I wanted to start my business. I wanted to get into property at that point. I had actually moved down south with my corporate job, and I had a flat in Manchester that I let out. The cashflow was really good and I thought that it was working really well. At the time, I was watching all the property programmes on TV and I loved them. That was the catalyst—realising that I could actually make some good money and it was almost all passive income. It was the realisation that I had to get into action and do something about that.

It was not through any deliberation on my part. I was just in the moment realising that it was working well. It took quite a long time to get to the stage where we invested in property. We did it eventually though, which is good.

A combination of fear and lack of knowledge had been holding me back from getting involved in property sooner. It was fear because it's a lot of money that you need in order to invest. I wondered what would happen if it went wrong. I thought, 'What if we don't know what we're doing?' I was definitely thinking about it too much. I wanted to have the knowledge to invest in property and to really understand what we were doing. So, both of those aspects were holding us back.

My first steps to move forward involved looking at the local market. We were back in Stockport at that point, so we thought we should have a look and see what was on the market. We checked how much properties were renting out for that you could buy for X amount of money. We tried to do some research into what we should be looking for in terms of the first property that we bought. We worked with a property mentor for a couple of months, and that experience gave us a little bit of confidence and helped us to understand what we were doing. He also helped us to negotiate a good deal on the property. So, the two main steps we took were doing the research and getting a property mentor.

Today, the main areas of my business are our portfolio and our website. I manage the small portfolio that we have by making sure that everything's taken care of on that side of things. We also launched a website called Just Do Property (www.JustDoProperty.co.uk) in 2010 that I still run today. We decided to start that because when we were back at the beginning, doing all our research, we couldn't find one place where we could go to get all of this information and help. From that, we figured that there was a gap in the market. And I wanted to do some additional work, aside from building our property portfolio. So, we decided to build and launch the Just Do Property website.

I built the website with my husband, Alec, who still works full-time as an IT consultant. So, it's just me running our property business, predominantly.) He helps with the technical aspects of the Just Do Property website when it gets a little too advanced for me, which is handy.

The website helps people starting off in property. We wanted, and want to, help them in every way that we can. So, we offer advice on what to do to get started. We like to update people on the news, what's going on in the market, what's going on with regards to the tax situation, the interest rates, and what strategies you can implement to build your property portfolio. We also have experts on our website to give guidance and support in their particular areas. You can click through and ask an expert for some advice. We offer lots of nice articles and downloads on there as well—many freebies. We like to give a lot of value to our subscribers.

The website keeps me very busy. I work full-time, but I also enjoy exercising, so I go to the gym three mornings a week, which I absolutely love. I take my girls to school and pick them up from school, and then I may carry on working in the evening. I'm full-time but I'm very flexible, which is what I love. I work from home. I can dip into things when I need to—it's brilliant.

We know a lot of people are using the website, because we get a lot of feedback. It's lovely to get that feedback when somebody needs help, to be able to offer advice to them or to point them to a resource, or to send them in the right direction. It's nice to have that interaction – it's proof that we've actually helped somebody to take a step forward. When you're experienced in something you don't realise everything you know. To help somebody with that knowledge is really nice.

It hasn't been completely smooth and easy along the way. The biggest challenge was trying to balance everything around my two daughters and actually starting a business. There was a lot to do and having that work-life balance was quite difficult. In the beginning, it was pretty hard. There were many times when I felt like giving up. Building a property portfolio, as many people know, is not easy. Building a business from scratch is not an easy undertaking at all. There were many times when I thought about going out and getting a job.

But every time I pulled back and stopped myself. I thought, 'who is going to let me go to the gym in the morning? Who Is going to let me spend days out with my kids. No one.' So, I persevered. I think if you've got a goal, you've got to keep going. It might not be quick to get there, but if you're consistent and take action every single day—little steps, baby steps—you will get there eventually. Definitely.

Other challenges to building our property portfolio have been the new government regulations which have made it very difficult. We have to change the way we do things now, and we need to understand everything. You can't really be an accidental landlord any more. Getting finance is a struggle as well. When we first started, it was very easy, but that's not the case any more. We've also had challenges with tenants. We've had horrendous nightmares with some tenants who just will not get out of the property. In those situations, we were not being paid and we had to go through the whole long process of getting them evicted. That's just awful because we were paying our mortgage—we were paying everything—and they're sitting in your property rent-free. That was absolutely terrible.

It seems surprising that people would do such a thing, but they don't think the same way as we do. They think they can get away with it, and they know how to play the system. But those people are very much the minority. For us, it was only one or two that caused us huge headaches. The rest of our tenants have been absolutely fantastic.

The big light bulb moment for me over the years was when I got that consistent income from property, and I understood how to do due diligence on a property in the right way. Understanding the research process was quite an 'aha' moment for me. Also, with our business, it's wonderful to see how it's grown, and to be able to give value to our subscribers, understanding that if we keep giving value the business will grow. That's just fabulous. The business is growing and the business is also helping people.

On our Just Do Property website, we do explain it as being like having your own virtual assistant collating all the most up-to-date property information. And I think that with the government changes more people are coming to our site for information. In the current climate, information and knowledge are power. You have to have those two things in order to move forward: either to get started on the property ladder or to build your property portfolio. It can be quite a risky business now if you don't understand all the legal requirements. We've got a legal requirements checklist on the homepage of our website, so investors can come and download that. There are five pages of legal requirements that you need to meet to make sure you are covered. I think a lot more people are coming to our website to get a better understanding. It's free, and it gives loads of value.

Some people may wonder why we aren't charging for this information and if it can be any good if we're not charging. Our website is free because we want to give people access to all the correct information. The information is extremely valuable, and it's a free resource for property investors.

We keep on top of new information day to day by using certain Google keywords, and by looking at what's going on in the news, going into the newspapers online and looking at what's going on in property. We have joined lots of different property groups to figure out what's happening in the industry and what's current. It is tricky to keep up to date, but if you have a process, it makes it much easier.

It's difficult to achieve that balance between being informed and being overwhelmed. We try to do one main newsletter each week which has a main bit of news about property during that week. We don't bombard people with information, but if there's something pertinent that week we'll focus on it. We'll blog about many other topics that are going on. But the key thing is our newsletter to our readers once a week.

I absolutely love showing other women that being a mum and running a business at the same time is achievable. I can show my daughters when they ask me what I do. I can tell them that I run this from home and we started this from scratch. I love talking to other female entrepreneurs too—whether they're in property or not—that do the same thing. As I mentioned, I go to the gym three times a week in the mornings, and many of the ladies at my gym are in a very similar position. They run their own business, but they run it from home in a flexible manner. The ability to actually do that is becoming quite prevalent, and it's wonderful.

The website has been my biggest success and achievement. We've got over 25,000 property investors on our list now who receive our information, and we built that from scratch. I'm really proud of it, and I'm really proud that it can actually help people get started in property.

We've had people share some of their accomplishments after using our resources. People come forward and say, 'Oh I didn't realise that was happening; thank you so much for letting me know about that'. Or it could be about a property that they've bought and it's been very successful for them. We've had a lot of people come forward and just say 'thank you' which makes it all worthwhile.

I like to help people who are just getting started. I would say that if you want to invest in property, just take that first step, do your research and get started. As I said before, we always wish we'd done it sooner. However, it's important to make sure that you do your research and due diligence on the property and the market. Do the groundwork. Call the letting agents and call the sales agents in that area. Find out everything you can about that property and the local market. Go and see the property as well. But don't over-analyse all the information. Remember that you make the money when you buy the property, not when you sell, so make sure you do the research. Make sure it's a good deal and that you buy at the right price. I think the top tip is just to get going with the right information.

Mistakes happen when people jump into deals that may not be the right thing for them. A hot deal might come through, but it's important to not just jump at something that looks good. We bought a few properties that we wish we hadn't bought, but they seemed like brilliant deals at that time. I wish we had taken a step back, and done all that research more thoroughly.

Recovering from buying something you wished you hadn't bought can be hard. There is one example I can think of for us that fortunately turned out fine, but we re-learnt the important lesson of going to see a place before purchasing it. We bought a deal from a company and it was a hot deal—lots of investors were excited about it—so we thought we'd grab it. We bought it and we were told it was a two-bedroom property. Then when we went to see it, it was a one-bedroom property. It wasn't actually worth what they said it was worth, but it still worked out because it was a good deal. We should have gone to see the property. When you're very busy and you're just getting started, and somebody says 'Oh you don't need to come see it,' that's a red flag. We should have gone to see that property. But it all worked out okay in the end.

I really believe in personal development, because it makes you personally responsible for your own positivity and focus. If you're building a property portfolio it can be quite hard to stay positive sometimes. There's a lot of negativity in the media. If you're working on yourself and your personal development through audio CDs or books I think that's really good. Invest in yourself as well, and be kind to yourself. Don't be negative about things that you've done. Try to keep a positive attitude. A little thing that I heard a couple of years ago is 'work smart, not hard'. I really like that. Sometimes you can be the hardest worker in the world and not actually get anywhere. In business and in property, if you work smart, you'll do really well.

Thinking positively is a key point for me. You can always—well, most of the time—turn a negative into a positive. I quite often think that some things are just meant to be. If you're not meant to get a deal, you won't get it. Try to turn each situation into a positive. Learn from what you've done, what mistakes you made and why you made them, and do something differently the next time. Life is a learning experience and we're not going to get everything right. Let's try to be positive about it and move forward.

AZIZ PATEL

I made a promise to buy my parents a home before my 18th birthday. It didn't matter how I was going to do it, but I just knew that it had to happen.

Active investor and developer with over two decades of commercial and real estate experience. Diverse residential and commercial portfolio in England and Wales. Motivational speaker, and author of "Property Auctions".

Services: Tailored property investment solutions. Wealth training and education. Coaching.
Email: info@azizpatel.com
Website: www.AzizPatel.com

In this chapter, I will share memories of going from feeling helpless, and lacking resources, to living a laptop lifestyle with my family today and enjoying the success, fulfilment and abundance created as a result of taking control of my financial future, whilst investing in my health and mindset.

This involved questioning and shifting my beliefs and attitude and making the impossible possible with small incremental steps in achieving the transition and transformations by setting small, medium and large goals. Also, using a vision board that I use on a daily basis, that I call: "Step Into Your Dreams".

My background is that we lived in Huddersfield, Yorkshire, on the ground floor; a two-bedroom council flat in a high-rise tower block. The structure was constructed after the Second World War, comprising of concrete and a rendered pebble-dash exterior and a perimeter-fenced garden.

My parents emigrated from India during the 1960s. My father was a civil servant and mother was a full-time homemaker. I was the youngest of four children. Whilst my other siblings were enjoying playing with their toys and friends growing up, I knew there was more to life than just having fun. On numerous occasions, it was embarrassing for our mother, when the local bailiffs would call at the door – they turned up asking for either the rent or threatening eviction. The last notice we received for eviction was just before my sixth birthday.

Unfortunately, my father was a 'spender' whilst my mother was a 'saver'. Neither of my parents has been exposed to financial education – similar to the majority of the world's population which has never received this either, i.e. understanding the fundamental difference between an asset and a liability and being in a position to take control of their finances.

My father, before he came to England, had a very prominent position and a well-paid, respected job in Bombay. Unfortunately, my late grandmother was diagnosed with tuberculosis and was bedridden in the hospital for over seven years. My grandfather also got diagnosed later with TB. My father had a high salary at the time, but it went into the hospital bills for his parents. So, whilst his relatives continued to sow the seeds of wealth, my father used the majority of his earnings to pay towards his parents' hospital bills and medication.

So, when he came to the UK, he was still dealing with the traumatic experience of coping with the aftermath, and later with the bereavement of his father, who died before I turned six. All of this was going on in the background, while my mother was looking after us, making sure that food was on the table and that we had a good upbringing based on traditional values. I wouldn't say we lived in poverty, but we were living close to the bread and butter line. There were no holidays or fancy excursions away. There was no going away overseas due to lack of extra money.

There was a wealthy side of my family, and a poor side of my family. My mother's side was wealthy though it felt to me like they adopted a "poor" mindset when it came to sharing. Everything was a secret when talking about business and money;

they were in business and loved to flash their cash. On the other hand, my father's side of the family were academic and valued education as a regarded foundation for the success of their position and family. They were abundant in nature and open to sharing their wisdom: doctors, lawyers, dentists.

Before my sixth birthday, and out of desperation rather than inspiration, I realised I had to look at other ways of making additional money to help my parents with outgoings in terms of savings and investments, rather than being a saver.

I grew up with the hand-me-down toys from others within my family or friends, so one day decided to get "creative" rather than '"angry". I had an idea with my best friend at the time. His name was Dean Steadman and he lived across the street with his parents in the same type of flat. I believed we could start trading unwanted toys, by creating a pop-up stall like the Saturday Market, but in our garden.

We had our own "pitch" in the garden. We sold toys to parents and kids who visited after seeing our creative posters in places in the neighbourhood and in local businesses which we distributed with the help of my siblings. We split the profit 50/50. We'd make enough to enjoy the profits and repeat for several months as a fun enterprise. It wasn't about making a huge shift in the world economy, though the challenge felt like it at the time. For us, it was just fun sharing this with other children and an adventure while it lasted.

We went from doing it every Saturday to then taking it into the playgrounds. The kids would donate their unwanted toys, and in exchange I would share 50 percent of the profit upon sale. The profits were used to invest in my new asset class and passion: stamps and collectable coins.

The flat we lived in had no central heating. There was no double-glazing or fancy appliances. The carpets we had were donated by a relative and were used before. The gadgets we had were also rented. They were the VCR and a Philips colour television. My parents even rented their telephone; it was one of those old green telephones where you'd have to dial and then it would rebound back to its original place when making an outgoing call. I still have the phone that we had back then, because I made the decision to do whatever it took to buy it instead of renting. Today, I use it more as a prop to give people an example of where this story began in comparison to where I am today.

The place we lived was an area you would call the urban fringe. It's the area where a lot of immigrants would live, and today if you look across the UK, you still have these pockets where immigrants have lived and they've either moved, evolved, or are still there. I told my parents we needed to move away from this area and to an environment that was positive for our family. It was me that came up with this idea, and I was only six, going on seven. My father realised that this was quite important because my mother began pushing: "Look, we need to leave this area for the kids' sake." We got offered this three-bed council house, but before we moved to the council house, I would help my brother with a paper delivery route and trading coins and stamps, to make sure that the person he was working for got the result they wanted. It wasn't about the money. It was my passion just to get out there and learn, because the environment at home was not very positive. While I had all the unconditional love I needed, I knew there was something missing, which was having a pot of money and having the freedom to choose what to do with it. So while I was saving up, it was either being given back to my mum for food, or used for immediate gratification.

When I visited my relatives in Manchester every other weekend via public transport with my mum, I saw the big divide in terms of wealth, the big difference between our so-called 'rich' relatives and 'us'. Each time we visited, the question asked by my cousins or aunts was; "How did you arrive here?" It was always the same answer: "We came on the bus." Although they wouldn't laugh in front of us, I suspected they were in hysterics in the background when they thought we were out of earshot. We didn't have a car; we only rented a car twice and that was for relatives' weddings.

My parents transitioned to a three-bedroom council house; a larger garden, a different environment when it came to attitudes and culture. It was during this period I met my first mentor, Carl Tipling, who was a very well-respected ex-police officer. I met him in the late 1980s after he had retired; he took me under his wing and gave me what I call a "check-up from the neck up" – he helped cure the "stinking thinking philosophies" and provided some positive nourishment and transformational interventions that radically expanded my vision for the future.

I would visit him frequently, observing his attitude, his demeanour, how he conducted himself, how he walked. "Just stand tall like a man does," he said. "You know, you might be a boy on the outside, but inside, you need to stand tall." He shared stories and insights, exposing me to positive and empowering messages.

I asked him what he used to read, and he shared with me: Dr. Vincent Peale, Winston Churchill, and many more. I was then exposed to *Messages* by Jim Rohn. I saw something in his hand, politely asking what it was as I was sweeping up in his garden, and he said, "Oh, it's a book. Would you like it?" He offered the book to me, and I was too embarrassed; I was very shy because I had a stutter in my voice and was near blind in one of my eyes. A doctor said I always had to wear an eye patch when growing up – I was ridiculed at school and always made fun of. I had to wear the chunky, nerdy spectacles and the hand-me-down clothes given to me by my elder siblings.

When the garments finally came down to me wearing them, they were either too short, too long, had the pleats in between, or had been bleached too many times. When I look back, it made me stronger, laying the foundations of strong family values, remaining humble and instilling the resilience to overcome adversity in a different way. Going to a school where the students were predominantly white gave me the edge from the training that I had up until the age of eight or nine. Using this as a catalyst, enabled me to apply competitiveness in sport – to take that into my education at school. But, with my mentor, I learned discipline from somebody with a military and policing background. He commanded a lot of respect in the community.

On some weekends, I'd go to Blackpool. Under the Blackpool Tower, there's a big store occupied today by a major retailer. As a child, I was shy. However, I could bring people to my cousins' stall where they would sell what today would be 99-pence items, but back then, they were 50 pence. So by the end of the day, there'd be hundreds and hundreds of 50-pence coins that had been collected. By the age of six I had decided that I never ever wanted to be in a position in which I had a home that would be a liability for my family. But I also knew I would have to trade money for time. So, I made a promise to buy my parents a home before my 18th birthday. It didn't matter how I was going to do it, but I just knew that before I turned 18 it had to happen. I remember feeling it was so far away, but then the number just left my head.

I remember my father buying a remote-controlled sports car for my birthday. Any other child would have fallen in love with a particular colour and model of car, but all I wanted was to buy a home for my parents so we'd never face these ordeals again. My father worked for over 60 years of his life, receiving a pension, but has not had the opportunity to travel and see the world enough to understand that we're financially blessed because of his sacrifice and being blessed to have amazing, supportive parents, regardless of our differences in values when it came to money.

He was proud and dignified in his own ways: he doesn't want any help from anyone, any hand-outs. He's just happy where he is and doing what he's doing. He takes responsibility for the life he's chosen.

Mentors are important. Mentors help catalyse the speed of a reaction or implementation, provided the individual is willing to be open-minded, eager, and have that grit inside and determination to follow through. Out of all my siblings, I'd probably say I'm the one who's probably had the most grit and faced adversity head-on.

Rather than getting angry or upset, let us instead ask, "How do we get through this? What can we do to make this easier?" You know, sometimes, we catch a deal in life with God. When you're in a state of gratitude, you attract more abundance – even when you don't have what you or others desire. I think, for myself, it was about appreciating what I had, being resourceful and utilising my surroundings. So, I wouldn't say I had a miserable life, but rather a very colourful, imaginative one.

My interest in property started at a very young age. At age five, looking across the garden, I saw this building that was a multiplex of flats occupied by tenants who were either claiming housing benefit or working, and I was in awe. I just thought, "Wow! This is so big. Wouldn't it be amazing to actually own the building?" And I asked my mum, "What would it take to own this building – the whole building?" My mum said, "You'd probably need £120,000 to buy it." And yes, the council actually gave the opportunity before the demolition was ordered to buy the entire building, because it was too expensive for them to renovate. This was in the 1990s, so that £120,000 one-off opportunity would probably be worth about £1.5 million today, in that part of Yorkshire.

It was only after Black Wednesday in the 1990s when things changed massively for the wider economy, but for me, it was from just before I turned six seeing this building and then listening to my father and mother argue when it came to finances.

My father is a humble person. He was the type to lend money to his friends, but he would rarely ask for the money loaned to be returned. He subscribed to magazines that offered very little value – and he would be the first person to register for various different competitions, some of which involved high-price tickets. The risk was high and it wasn't a calculated one.

Seeing that experience, I knew we had to have a safety net. It was only when I was attending high school that one of our neighbours in the area by chance was selling their house.

She became terminally ill, and they were about to put their property on the market, and I had that "light bulb" or "aha" moment. I thought, "Wow! Wouldn't it be great if I could sell this property for you!" They had recently instructed a local agent who'd been out and given an evaluation. What I did was to cheekily use the power of the Internet to see if I could market this property on a search engine. Back then, before the days of Lycos and Yahoo, I put the property on the search engine ad listing, and actually had people responding to it. All I could think was, "Wow! I actually have people contacting me via email for a property in England." I did not have the owner's permission, but I just took the initiative and did it with no image, only text. It was very simple. I put the price that she wanted on there, and even had people from the U.S. contacting me. There was one person who contacted me who was interested because they had a relative in another part of Yorkshire, but wanted to buy a property in the specific area to keep it in their family's history.

I thought it was quite honourable and it was then that I got intrigued.

On a Monday, I'd do cross-country, and would have to wait for the bus to get home from school. So, I had access to the computers in the rooms where some of the kids had detentions. I thought that rather than doing what the other kids were doing – learning to connect an email and message penpals – I wanted to see how I could learn more about this. So, I went deeper into it, and it was by chance that I then understood that there was a market for people who needed to sell their home. Again, it came from the U.S., from when I was searching online. I noticed lots of people on many different websites – this was back in the early 1990s. I searched for the domain name housesbought.co.uk and it was available. I was the first to register that domain.

By the fourth year, I became quite well known in athletics, particularly in running, because of my competitive nature. Although I struggled to speak in front of the class, I had that creative ability. I got interested in property on the weekends, but I knew it wasn't what I was going to do because my mother elected for me to become a doctor. That was her big vision: "My son, who's the youngest of the family – he'll become a doctor." She didn't have a strategy for how I was going to do it; she just told everyone that her son was going to be a doctor and that was the end of it.

Despite my parents' best efforts and expectations of me, I knew subconsciously that what I wanted to do was to be involved with property, and it had something to do with helping people.

I used my knowledge of the computer and people, and started collecting lots and lots of paper – hundreds and thousands of reams of paper, the old-school kind with the perforated lines to tear it. I would get a marker pen and write things like, "Stinks of weed? Think of me." Then, as I got a little bit older, I got more creative and wrote things like – "Smells of poo, I'll buy too," and "If you know anyone selling a smelly house, call."

As I got more confident in my teenage years, I started to utilise the library and pledged to help them out if they'd let me use their copier. My brother and sister were at the polytechnic at Huddersfield – I'd ask them for paper. They'd give me paper, and I'd ask my brother, who is four years my senior, to give me any paper he could because I was limited in terms of money and wanted to leverage what I had saved up, which was by then just over £2,000. I had also already built up a stamp collection worth over £1,500. To this day, I still have the majority of the stamps and coins.

At that time I had a job doing newspaper deliveries, with two routes, one in the morning and one in the afternoon. For the morning round, every newspaper I would post through the door I'd scrunch up my own flyer and chuck it through the letterbox with my fingers covered in black ink. I got fired from one or two paper rounds because the neighbours complained that someone was throwing rubbish through the letterbox, but that didn't stop me. Then, as I gathered more momentum, I started to create stickers for pizza boxes and asked pizza companies if they could deliver the pizzas and include my stickers on there. And they did it for free. They were more than happy – they saw my eagerness for what I was doing. I think it was in 1996 that I had a lightbulb moment of setting up a student agency for property. Thus a

Student Letting portal was born, one of the first online search engines for accommodation.

In 1997, I saw a detached Victorian house, opposite the park for sale. I didn't know how I was going to buy, but as a child I knew that the house that my parents would live in would have to be opposite a park, and it'd have to have tennis courts nearby because I loved playing tennis. It would have a huge field so I could play football. The home would have to be close to town so I could go to the shops and visit friends.

I didn't know how I was going to do it, but in 1997, the property I had visualised came to auction, complete with crystal chandeliers. So, I dragged my mother on the bus on a cold, wet, spring evening and took her to the auction. The hammer fell down, and I was shaking. As the hammer fell, I looked to my left, to my right, and I twisted my head like an owl all the way to the back to see who had won the bid on the property. The auctioneer looked me in the eye – his name was Raymond Butterworth, he's retired now – and he said, "Lot number, Sir, what's your lot number?" I was still trying to catch my breath, thinking, "What in the hell? What's he talking about?" The property had never had a survey done, I'd viewed it once and had told my mother, "This is the house that we'll live in." I didn't have a clue how I was going to raise the money in 28 days. The hammer fell down; I was under contract. Under the age of 18, I had to sign the contract, and had to be driven home because I didn't even have a cheque book; I had to ask my sister to write a cheque, even though the full sum was not in her account, so that she could pay the 10 percent plus the admin fee. As soon as I went out of the auction,

I put £1 in the phone box and rang my uncle, an entrepreneur at the time, and said to him, "Look, I've just bid on an auction property, and Mum told me to ring you. Can you help?" Anyway, he put the phone down – he just thought it was stupid – and before we knew it, all of my mother's family knew what I had just done. Fast forward a month later and I had pulled through in spite of the odds.

My parents still live in the house that I bid for back in 1997.

This was the exact house that I dreamed about as a child – I'd told my friends quietly that when I got older, this was where I was going to live, and they never believed me. I was fired up. So fired up that my confidence, my ability and what I learned in my previous years kicked in. My mum said to me, "I want you to be a doctor." And I said, "It's not going to happen." She said, "I don't care what you say. You're going to have change your plans." But despite what my mother said, I took a year out. I rushed through my exams and fast-tracked just to keep her happy. I did six months of work in about seven weeks and decided to take a gap year, travel around Europe, and focus on what I wanted to do when I got back.

While my mother was happy, she was gutted that I would not go down the medical route. But despite being blind in one eye, I knew I would not let anything become a disadvantage. I had a few accidents throughout my teenage years. One was splitting my head open; I had to have six stitches, lost nearly a pint of blood and luckily escaped suffering a haemorrhage affecting my long-term memory.

Despite all this, I still wanted to plod through. So, when I went to university, I studied and I got my gap year. But while studying, I knew I couldn't take out a student loan because of what I'd learned, and what I'd been exposed to when it came to investing for financial security and being resourceful.

My business philosophy was simple in the early 1990s and is kept simple till this day. We keep things really straightforward so people understand. When they need help, we step in and help them and we show them how we help them with a range of ethical solutions. We give them the solution. They have a choice of whether they want to step over that bridge with the solution, and if they do, they get the answers they need. We acquire the asset and either sell or develop it. What I was doing back in the 1990s was sourcing and flipping, from charging £5 a lead, which was a name – contact details of somebody who needed to sell a house – right up £200 a lead, which was still quite a lot of money. But the investor would buy a house that was probably worth about £15,000 for maybe £11,000 or £12,000, and be able to turn it around, sell it for a profit and make around £8,000 or £9,000 after completing the renovation work within a period of four to five months. This was before the six-month rule – buy-to-let mortgages came to the market in 1998.

It was in my university years that I realised that people who buy property to rent out need somebody to manage it. I noticed the standard of accommodation at polytechnics, which were re-institutionalised to university status. The new universities began attracting investment from overseas, with a lot more students from newer pastures.

The standard of quality rental accommodation was increasing for halls of residence and the larger PLC organisations/institutions, so I wanted to take my business model from being an online student agency to create a boutique, real-life, fully-fledged office. I took on the business from my bedroom. Even though I was travelling overseas, I could still operate the business without having to be at an office, but a company was created by two friends who were studying nearby at the time. Rather than compete, I decided to reform our business – to let them do what they were doing and to create the first agency that dealt only with students in the region.

"Generalists make a living. Specialists make a fortune"

That business grew so much in two years. While I was working towards my degree, I then ended up investing in other ventures; one of those was a gentlemen's barbershop. Somebody made a mistake during my hair cut and I set a goal that I'd open up a barber's business within six weeks. It was a foolish idea, but four weeks later, I opened up a shop called Jester's Barber Studio just to make fun of the guy who didn't quite make my hair look the way I wanted it.

Within in a period of four years, while studying at university, I'd already travelled through Europe. I'd be going to destinations in Cannes, France, Spain, to meet property investors on, say, Friday, and be back to university on the Monday morning, for the lecture. My friends would ask me, "Where did you go last weekend?" "What did you do?" I'd say, "Well, it's been one of those weekends." How to explain? They'd say, "Oh, did you have a lot on?" I'd say, "Yeah, there's a lot going on," but not tell them much at all. "Did you have a lot to do, uni work?" I'd reply, "Yeah, you know what it's like." But they wouldn't know that I had been on a yacht and private plane less than 48 hours ago. I was enjoying the rewards of success in business and relationships created with successful developers and entrepreneurs.

Within a period of four years, I had expanded our agency to three offices. I had over a dozen staff, and a chain of hair and beauty salons. I did not have a single clue about how to barber or blow-dry, yet we were selling many leading hair care and beauty products, and I even got invited to meet one of the partners of Toni & Guy. So, I got to meet people in these circles, and they got involved in investing in different businesses.

In 2003, I was offered the opportunity to meet Sir Richard Branson and be part of The Entrepreneurs' Forum, along with other fellow entrepreneurs, in Newcastle. So, my story went from acquiring the property for my parents to becoming a well-connected and young entrepreneur amongst my peers and property/business community.

Unfortunately, when you're in business, you face competition and adversity as life will catch you on the 'blind-side'. Our business was competing with university accommodation from which clients came to us, because even though we were charging more, we were offering a better-valued service. The properties we had received instruction for were letting faster. We were getting increased rentals, and business was expanding exponentially. There were minimal voids. I was taking on commercial contracts on large buildings that were previously contracted out to asylum seekers through the UK Home Office.

Previously, refugees who fled Iran in the 1990s for asylum in the UK would be living in such buildings. When their contracts came to an end. These buildings soon became empty. I stepped in and grasped the opportunities in areas of Sunderland, Newcastle and Middlesbrough, and signed up the legal paperwork, revamping the buildings in stages with light refurbishment work and using my money and borrowings to take them on five- or ten-year leases. We would let out to university students, the landlord would receive a fixed amount of guaranteed income and we would pocket the difference.

So, as the business continued to grow, the money was reinvested back in. However, at one point it seemed that for every pound that was being deposited via the bank; fifty pence was being debited. I was a bit naïve, and inexperienced at the time, having not understood correct operating procedures, measuring KPI's weekly, to systemising the business, streamlining, and putting procedures in place so that the company could follow a code of practice. I was brilliant in sales and marketing and dealing with management duties, but unfortunately, I didn't have the technical ability and business acumen to ensure the financials were up to standard.

In 2004, I reached a focal point where I looked at my bank balance and realised there were huge gaps. When I saw where money was being siphoned off to, I knew there was something off. Everything I did was online, and I realised something wasn't right – my cheque-books and accounts were accounted for. But then I realised the discrepancy was over £180,000 within a successive period of about six or seven months.

"You will fail your way to success, but don't give up if you are to grow and learn from these lessons called life".

Some would say I was a sucker and foolish for not looking through my accounts and reconciling everything by hiring a bookkeeper. It was an expensive lesson learned earlier in life that you've got to let things go and take them as lessons.

I used this as a foundation for living the quality of life I do today. When I look back, that was the greatest opportunity and lesson because it happened at such a young age.

Things were still very difficult for me, however. At the time, I was raising money for Marie Curie Cancer charity, participating in the famous Great North Run, raising tens of thousands of pounds for a worthy cause. I made the intention to raise the profile of cancer awareness in the region, having lost my cousin to Leukaemia during the period whilst I was living in this bubble. I felt the calling to run in his memory.

What you focus on, is what you will attract. The week after, my father was unwell, my mother was later diagnosed with diabetes, and my brother was also undergoing treatment for depression. While all of this was going on, I was living 150 miles away, working 18-hour days, seven days a week.

It was only during a moment of intervention with a colleague, that I had an epiphany moment at my cleaning company, which was a spin-off venture. We had cleaning contracts outsourced by the local authority to work on social housing. I recall being on all fours because a member of staff was off sick. This was to fulfil a promise to the client previously to ensure that a one-off job would get completed.

I was dealing with a full office block that needed to be cleaned.

I was on all fours after having driven out to buy vacuum cleaners at Argos because we didn't have enough equipment, and I remember a guy looking me in the eye as I was cleaning. He said, "Aziz. You can make money, or make excuses, but you can't have both." And I thought, "Wow! Where did that come from?"

He just stopped me in my tracks. At that moment, I just thought, "Right – I need to finish what I'm doing. I need to let the staff go." My mum wasn't in a good place, neither was my brother,

I had a sink-hole with my bank account, and my head was still between my legs living like a river that runs through Egypt called "Denial" (I know it may appear misspelt but think about the context). I was being 'too masculine' and feeling macho by not showing my emotions on the outside – I was hurt on the inside.

So I told my parents upon arriving to visit after a two-hour drive, "Look, I've got to go back tomorrow. I've got to return. I've got a huge diary of events and commitments pre-planned." And they agreed reluctantly though they wanted me to stay. They said, "Look, we really want you to pack up everything and live with us." Up to that point, they did not know about anything I had amassed in terms of resourcefulness, friends, assets, investments, equity etc.

I had created a monster. There were over a dozen staff, three offices, four different businesses. But my parents didn't know what was going on. So when I pulled up home in a big car my mum gave me a slap, before asking; "Where did you get the money to buy that car?" I said, "Mum, I've worked." And she said, "Don't lie, okay?" She was dreading what every parent would not want their child to do, "Don't lie. Just tell me where you got it." So I had to explain what happened, and I thought,

"Oh, no, I'm going to have to explain everything – what's good, and then, what's not so good."

Having explained myself over dinner, I felt emotionally drained, returning on the M1, but I left the car – I had a van that had been parked for a few weeks. I thought, "I'm going to go up in the van. It's time to pack up some of these things and bring them back." So, I was on the M1, just heading onto the M62 towards North Yorkshire, and the vehicle broke down without warning; it was the timing belt that snapped. At this moment, I realised that it was time to just wind things up, and move back. Sitting on the hard shoulder facing reality, I knew from deep within that this was God's message for me to spend time with the people that meant the most.

I made the bold decision, and soon fell into depression for over four weeks, though it felt like years. I locked myself in the office that I had created after I came back from my holidays and it was my only escape, my sanctuary. In those four weeks, it was the blame game, crying and feeling the pain of guilt and shame. I cannot go into the full detail of everything that happened for legal reasons. But suffice to say that I lay on the floor staring at the ceiling whilst thinking in darkness and silence of all the reasons I hated the person who had siphoned off the money from my business.

Then, I spent three weeks blaming myself for everything. Then, moving into the fifth week, I just thought, "Come on. How do I get through this? Look back at what you've done – how did you get there?" I listened to a track – it was an Arabic track – and some stranger, for some unknown reason, had sent me a link, which wasn't meant to go to me. I looked at it and it was an artist, a singer, just singing in Arabic. It was, "Mother," by the artist Sami Yusuf; his mother's gone, she's left the world, but he's reminiscing and missing his mother so much that he's crying in the song.

I realised I was not in a bad place in comparison. I'm standing in a seven-bedroom, detached house, with chandeliers hanging over me, and I'm thinking, "Come on. You could be in a lot worse place. You're in a great place. Be grateful at least." I got outside and started walking, and I started to look at the park where I dreamed of living as a kid, and I walked and walked.

When my father first arrived, he came in 1963 on a ship. He had £5 to his name. He walked from Dewsbury and ended up in Huddersfield, which is a good two-and-a-half-hour walk. Well, I walked for about four hours that evening. I thought that regardless of what happened, I'd have people who were going to be angry and blame me. From one minute managing all their properties, to now returning them all, they were going to be upset, because someone had to pick up the pieces and manage the property. I had to face all of that and was in a very bad place, even suicidal at one point.

I wasn't in debt. I didn't owe anyone any money, but I'd made verbal promises, and I'd made written promises to people guaranteeing their rent. They were not company guarantees, they were personal guarantees.

So, I thought, "I can't hide from all this. I've got to deal with all of this." I thought, "I've got to do something. Otherwise, I'm going to go crazy." I had had many different labouring jobs, from working in a pizza place to working on a landfill site, right through to working on a production line, to promoting bars and clubs, to working in a bank for Barclays, and training customers. I had worked for multi-level marketing firms and spoken on platforms. I just thought, "I need to do something with my life – rather be a Jack of all trades and master of none – by mastering time."

I took a pizza job. I thought, "I've got to get outside the home because I can't feel sorry for myself." The environment at home was not good. My brother was unwell and nobody knew what to do or how to deal with it. All I could think was, "I've got to take this job." So, I took a part-time job and within two weeks, the owner knew there was a quality that he saw in me that maybe I didn't, and he told me, "You're too qualified for this position. What do you do?" I didn't want my past to come out – I had to keep that locked down because I was just the guy that delivered pizzas. But he couldn't understand why every customer that I met would tip me so much.

He said, "I don't understand. I pay you a wage, but how do you get paid more than double from what I'm paying you?" I said, "I don't know. I really don't know the answer." So, he asked me to take him through it, and then he told me, "I've got a portfolio of properties, and I've heard that you were previously involved in rentals. Can you help?" I said, "I'd love the opportunity." It was in that moment that I said to myself, "I've got to get out. I've got to do what I've done before, I've got to follow my vision of what I did with the business I had."

So, I politely asked my sister, who was at the time enjoying what I considered a high-paying corporate position, to leave her job. I was still feeling down and lonely and depressed about what was going on, so I said, "I want to set up a business, and in five years' time, I want you to run it. It's going to be hard work, but it will be worth it. What do you think?" It was a very weak pitch but she saw something in it, and she bought into the idea. The business grew and grew and it's still a continued success today. The legacy continues because of the decision not to think small and to pursue a bigger vision

I ended up staying for longer than five years, but before I even launched the business my past came to haunt me. In business, there's no such thing as a transparent transaction, even when you're buying and selling fruit, because if your intentions are good, the other person may not have the same intentions as you. Accusations and stories arose to discredit my name and reputation, but all I could say to my sister was, "We're just going to have to ride through this storm." I had been using the same brand I had used since my teens and couldn't accept the idea of changing it – it would have been like Virgin changing its name. So, I stuck by it.

My sister stood by me entirely and made a massive sacrifice, leaving her career as an accountant, but it was worth it in the end. Today, the firm Student Haven is still adding value to the masses and is the No.1 student agency in Huddersfield, West Yorkshire.

I started to show people how to buy property, before, during, and after auction, using the skills I had acquired since 1997. I got actively involved in auctions throughout the North East, and Yorkshire, and different parts of England. I was driving everywhere. I'd sign a contract on paper and sell it the next day to an investor. After I departed, I told my sister that now was the time I wanted to carry my vision forward of becoming a developer and growing in scale. So, that's when I then started to use my skillset to share my experience through auctions, whilst working with joint-venture partners and buying buildings, converting them, and renting them out. That's where we are today.

To invest in property and achieve what it takes, you first need to overcome your fear. I believe that before you can overcome the fear with the mind-set, it's necessary to understand the other person. In other words, you must get to know the person because you're not necessarily investing money in the asset, you're investing in them and with them.

The three things to look out for when hiring or intending to do a joint venture / partnership are: energy, integrity and intelligence. Any person you're investing in must have a certain level of energy and they must have a certain level of integrity. Integrity, rather than being a word, is based on how you execute yourself in what you're doing; it's part of who you are. Anyone you invest in must also have a certain level of intelligence. Regardless of where the property markets are moving, when you've got the three combined, you get the result quicker. It's as simple as that. In today's market, as an investor, to keep up to date on what you're doing and your head above the water, you need to understand the motive of the person you're investing in. What are they aspiring to achieve, and what have they achieved before arriving at where they are today? Energy, intelligence, and integrity, in no particular order.

Before you invest, ask yourself whether they have an exit, and if they don't I would be worried. If I'm going into a house, I need to know where the windows and doors are. And if I'm exiting, why am I investing in property? What's my reason to? Am I looking at a sort of short-term, quick turnaround? You've got to be aligned with that particular investor.

I had a conversation with an investor from a very similar heritage to my parents. He was a bit surprised that there was another fellow Gujarati (that's the native mother tongue language we speak). My name, Patel, means "land of the farmers". So, ironically, my ancestors, including my grandfather, owned a lot of land: they had many hectares of it. But over the years, unfortunately because of corruption and politics, that land disappeared. To this day my uncles have land and property, but my father never inherited any of it. He moved to the UK and said, "I don't want anything to do with it. I'm not going to go back. I'm going to stay here for the kids."

Knowing that when we leave this planet, we leave behind everything, had really impacted and empowered me to shape the lives of others including our family. We're merely the temporary guardians to the property we hold or control on behalf of our kids.

But from an investment point of view, if I'm investing in you, I need to know what your exit is. I need to know concisely what it is you're striving to achieve, and whether your values align with my own.

The person I mentioned of a similar Gujarati heritage was wealthy and rich. They had seen a project I shared online and had £1,250,000 to invest from their common investment syndicate that held just under £20 million. But within 15 minutes of our conversation, I established that their values were not aligned with ours: they were looking to play at high stakes for high profit over a short period. I confirmed during our brief conversation, politely, that their business model would not be compatible with ours.

However, I frequently get asked and challenge myself to source a solution in these situations by connecting with someone suitable. As an investor, the more you say no, the more you give yourself the opportunity to focus on the important things in life with higher purpose. Learn to say "no" when necessary, without saying, "no." For example, someone comes to you and asks, "What do you think of this? Would you invest with me? Would you think I'm investable?" You have to say to them they have a really good idea, "but right now is not an ideal time and maybe when you have a bit more experience you should come back to me with a proposal."

This method is more empowering because a lot of people today find it very difficult to accept or even grasp rejection. Just watch *The Apprentice* and you'll see that those of today's generation – the Millennials – are very impatient. They're used to things moving very quickly. They want answers quickly. If you get a text message and don't respond to it, they get frustrated because they're not used to patience. It pays dividends in the long term to remain patient and steadfast when possible.

You also need to go where the money is obviously, but overall, with any business you enter it is important to have a strong exit. Otherwise, you're going to get stuck.

I have written a book called *Property Auctions – 7 Steps To Financial Freedom* as an aid to help people interested in this exciting and proven strategy to wealth, freedom and profit. It gives the reader fundamentals, removes the mess, and helps any investor who wants to get their foot on the property ladder, enlarge their portfolio, giving them a deeper insight into how the world of auctions works. It goes over the ABCs right through to the Zs, where they can acquire property before, during and after auction, right through to strategies that many investors are not aware of, as well as what to avoid. So, actually reading through the book and applying the seven steps will help you as a reader to create your own bank vault, regardless of your financial situation, even if your credit's impaired, whatever your background, regardless of which country or nationality you are, and your experience.

The distance between where you are and where you want to be is "your reasons or excuses". So let me ask you a question after reading this:

"When would you like to schedule our call so we can make this happen?"

The time is NOW... Not yesterday or tomorrow...

WWW.POWERHOUSEPUBLISHING.COM

Printed in Great Britain
by Amazon